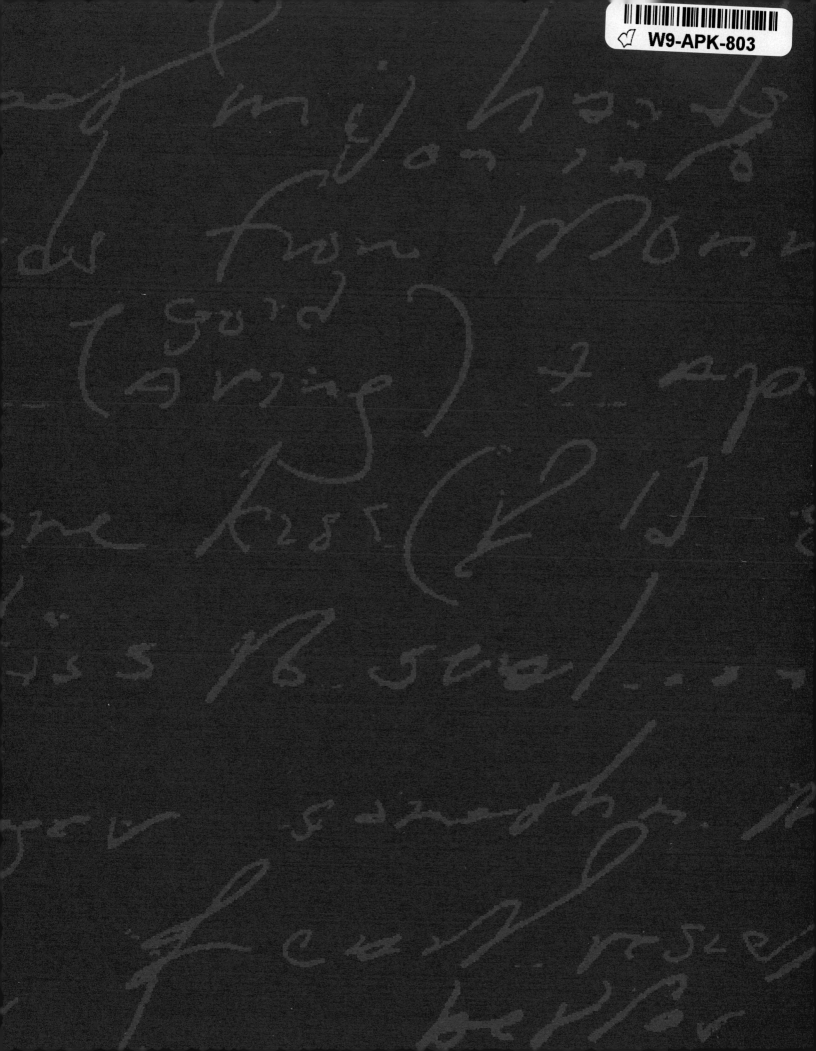

BRUCE SPRINGSTEEN

SONGS

BRUCE SPRINGSTEEN
SONGS

AVON BOOKS  NEW YORK

Copyright © 1998 by Bruce Springsteen
Project Director: Sandra Choron
Editor: Robert Santelli
Design: Sandra Choron, Harry Choron
Management: Jon Landau Management

AVON BOOKS, INC.
1350 Avenue of the Americas
New York, New York 10019

Visit our website at **http://www.AvonBooks.com**
ISBN: 0-380-97619-6

Library of Congress Cataloging in Publication Data:

Springsteen, Bruce.
   [Songs.   Texts.   Selections]
   Bruce Springsteen songs.
        p.   cm.
   1. Rock music—Texts.   I. Title.
   ML54.6.S79B7 1998   98-35197
   782.42166' 0268—dc21   CIP
                                               MN

First Avon Books Printing: December 1998

AVON TRADEMARK REG. U.S. PAT. OFF. AND IN OTHER COUNTRIES, MARCA REGISTRADA, HECHO EN U.S.A.

Printed in the U.S.A.

FIRST EDITION

QPK   10 9 8 7 6 5 4 3 2 1

In memory of Douglas Springsteen
1924–1998

contents

greetings from asbury park, n.j.

blinded by the light

growin' up

mary queen of arkansas

does this bus stop at 82nd street?

lost in the flood

the angel

for you

spirit in the night

it's hard to be a saint in the city

At twenty, in my parents' apartment in San Mateo, California

n 1971, after years of playing music in high school gyms, beach clubs, and bars up and

down the New Jersey Shore, I found myself at a crossroads. The local music scene was

overflowing with Top 40 cover bands. There wasn't a lot of interest in hearing original

music, which is what I mainly played. At twenty-one, I already had a good deal of local

success, playing to as many as three thousand people at my own shows. My band Steel

Mill and I had done it all without a recording contract. But my first trip to California with the band

had opened me up to new musical ideas. Upon returning home, I changed musical direction and

began to perform under my own name. But now it'd gotten hard to find steady work playing my own

songs with a band. I decided I was going to write some music to survive on with just myself and the

guitar.

One day a former manager and friend, Carl "Tinker" West, drove by my house in Highlands, New Jersey. I was sitting on the front steps. He shouted through the car window that he was going up to New York City. He had met a music publisher named Mike Appel and why didn't I take the ride with him and play him a few songs? I grabbed my guitar and hopped into Tinker's car and a couple of hours later met Mike. After he heard some music, he said he was interested in working with me, wanted to publish my songs, and together we'd see where it might lead.

I'd been going through some hard times in New Jersey for a while, and I planned, once again, to leave the state. Plus, I had heard plenty of promises before. So I left that day telling Mike I was interested, but without making a commitment. That Christmas, Tinker and I drove cross country to California. I visited my folks and spent several months trying to make a living as a musician in the Bay Area. It didn't work out. There were too many good musicians, and I'd left my rep as "bar band king" in Jersey. So it was back home for me. I did a few gigs at the Shore with the band for seed money and made a call to Mike Appel in New York City. I met Mike's partner, Jim Cretecos, and they signed me to an exclusive recording, publishing, and management deal.

Though I'd never known anyone who had made a professional record, I knew two things: one, I wanted to sign to a record company as a solo artist—the music I'd been writing on my own was more individual than the material I'd been working up with my bands. The independence of being a solo performer was important to me. And two, I was going to need a good group of songs if I ever did get the chance to record.

I went home and started to work on the songs for *Greetings from Asbury Park, N.J.* They were written in a style that had developed out of my earlier acoustic writing. From the late '60s on, I

With John Hammond

always had a notebook full of acoustic songs. I'd do the occasional coffeehouse, but mostly that

material went unused. The songs required too much attention for a crowded bar on a Saturday

night.

I did most of my writing in the back of a closed beauty salon on the floor beneath my apart-

ment in Asbury Park. There I had an Aeolian spinet piano my aunt had given me, and amidst the

old hairdryers and washing sinks, I wrote the songs that comprised *Greetings*.

Greetings was the only album where I wrote the lyrics first, setting them to music later. I'd

write the verses, then pick up the guitar or sit at the piano and follow the inner rhythm of the

words. I traveled to New York City on the bus, trying whatever I'd written latest out on Mike and

Jimmy. They were enthusiastic, so I kept on plugging.

Most of the songs were twisted autobiographies. "Growin' Up," "Does This Bus Stop," "Blinded by the Light," "Spirit in the Night," "For You," "Lost in the Flood," "Saint in the City" found their seed in people, places, hang-outs, and incidents I'd seen and things I'd lived. I wrote impression-istically and changed names to protect the guilty. I worked to find something that was identifiably mine.

After a few disappointing auditions, Mike talked his way into Columbia Records, and I was signed by the legendary A&R man John Hammond and Clive Davis, president of the label. We cut *Greetings* in three weeks. But Clive handed it back and said there was nothing that could be played on the radio. I'm glad he did; I went home and wrote "Blinded by the Light" and "Spirit in the Night." With the previously missing Clarence Clemons on saxophone, these songs were recorded, and the record was finished.

I never wrote in that style again. Once the record was released, I heard all the "new Dylan" comparisons, so I steered away from it. But the lyrics and spirit of *Greetings* came from a very unselfconscious place. Your early songs come out of a moment when you're writing with no sure prospect of ever being heard. Up until then, it's just you and your music. That only happens once.

b l i n d e d   b y   t h e   l i g h t

Madman drummers, bummers and
   Indians in the summer with a
   teenage diplomat
In the dumps with the mumps as
   the adolescent pumps his way into
   his hat
With a boulder on my shoulder, feelin'
   kinda older, I tripped the merry-go-
   round
With this very unpleasing sneezing and
   wheezing the calliope crashed to the
   ground
Some all-hot half-shot was headin' for
   the hot spot snappin' his fingers,
   clappin' his hands
And some fleshpot mascot was tied
   into a lover's knot with a whatnot in
   her hand
And now young Scott with a slingshot
   finally found a tender spot and
   throws his lover in the sand
And some bloodshot forget-me-not
   whispers "Daddy's within earshot
   save the buckshot, turn up the band"

And she was blinded by the light
Cut loose like a deuce, another runner
   in the night
Blinded by the light
She got down but she never got tight
   but she'll make it all right

Some brimstone baritone anticyclone

rolling stone preacher from the East
He says "Dethrone the dictaphone, hit it
   in its funny bone, that's where they
   expect it least"
And some new-mown chaperone was
   standin' in the corner all alone
   watchin' the young girls dance
And some fresh-sown moonstone was
   messin' with his frozen zone to
   remind him of the feeling of romance

Yeah he was blinded by the light
Cut loose like a deuce, another runner
   in the night
Blinded by the light
He got down but he never got tight but
   he's gonna make it tonight

Some silicone sister with her manager's
   mister told me I got what it takes
She said "I'll turn you on sonny to
   something strong if you play that
   song with the funky break"
And go-cart Mozart was checkin' out the
   weather chart to see if it was safe to
   go outside
And little Early-Pearly came by in her
   curly-wurly and asked me if I needed
   a ride
Oh some hazard from Harvard was
   skunked on beer playin' backyard
   bombardier
Yes and Scotland Yard was trying hard,

they sent some dude with a calling
   card, he said "Do what you like but
   don't do it here"
Well I jumped up, turned around, spit in
   the air, fell on the ground
Asked him which was the way back
   home
He said "Take a right at the light, keep
   goin' straight until night and then
   boy you're on your own"
And now in Zanzibar a shootin' star
   was ridin' in a sidecar hummin' a
   lunar tune
Yes and the avatar said blow the bar
   but first remove the cookie jar, we're
   gonna teach those boys to laugh
   too soon
And some kidnapped handicap was
   complainin' that he caught the
   clap from some mousetrap he bought
   last night
Well I unsnapped his skullcap and
   between his ears I saw a gap but
   figured he'd be all right

He was just blinded by the light
Cut loose like a deuce, another runner
   in the night
Blinded by the light
Mama always told me not to look into
   the sights of the sun
Oh but mama that's where the fun is

Opposite: New York City, 1972

growin' up

I stood stonelike at midnight suspend-
　　ed in my masquerade
I combed my hair till it was just right
　　and commanded the night brigade
I was open to pain and crossed by the
　　rain and I walked on a crooked
　　crutch
I strolled all alone through a fallout
　　zone and came out with my soul
　　untouched
I hid in the clouded wrath of the crowd
　　but when they said "Sit down" I
　　stood up
Ooh . . . growin' up

The flag of piracy flew from my mast,
　　my sails were set wing-to-wing
I had a jukebox graduate for first
　　mate, she couldn't sail but she sure
　　could sing
I pushed B-52 and bombed 'em with
　　the blues with my gear set stubborn
　　on standing
I broke all the rules, strafed my old

high school, never once gave thought
　　to landing
I hid in the clouded warmth of the
　　crowd but when they said "Come
　　down" I threw up
Ooh . . . growin' up

I took month-long vacations in the
　　stratosphere and you know it's really
　　hard to hold your breath
I swear I lost everything I ever loved or
　　feared, I was the cosmic kid in full
　　costume dress
Well my feet they finally took root in the
　　earth but I got me a nice little place
　　in the stars
And I swear I found the key to the
　　universe in the engine of an old
　　parked car
I hid in the mother breast of the crowd
　　but when they said "Pull down" I
　　pulled up
Ooh . . . growin' up
Ooh . . . growin' up

mary queen of arkansas

Mary queen of Arkansas, it's not too
   early for dreamin'
The sky is grown with cloud seed sown
   and a bastard's love can be
   redeeming
Mary, my queen, your soft hulk is
   reviving
No you're not too late to desecrate, the
   servants are just rising

Well I'm just a lonely acrobat, the live
   wire is my trade
I've been a shine boy for your acid brat
   and a wharf rat of your state
Mary, my queen, your blows for freedom
   are missing
You're not man enough for me to hate or
   woman enough for kissing

The big top is for dreamers, we can take
   the circus all the way to the border
And the gallows wait for martyrs whose
   papers are in order

But I was not born to live to die and you
   were not born for queenin'
It's not too late to infiltrate, the servants are just leavin'

Mary queen of Arkansas, your white
   skin is deceivin'
You wake and wait to lie in bait and you
   almost got me believin'
But on your bed Mary I can see the
   shadow of a noose
I don't understand how you can hold me
   so tight and love me so damn loose

But I know a place where we can go
   Mary
Where I can get a good job and start
   out all over again clean
I got contacts deep in Mexico where the
   servants have been seen

does this bus stop at 82nd street?

Hey bus driver keep the change, bless
    your children, give them names
Don't trust men who walk with canes
Drink this and you'll grow wings on
    your feet
Broadway Mary, Joan Fontaine,
    advertiser on a downtown train
Christmas crier bustin' cane
He's in love again

Where dock workers' dreams mix with
    panthers' schemes to someday own
    the rodeo
Tainted women in Vistavision perform
    for out-of-state kids at the late show

Wizard imps and sweat-sock pimps,
    interstellar mongrel nymphs

Rex said that lady left him limp
Love's like that (sure it is)
Queen of diamonds, ace of spades,
    newly discovered lovers of the
    everglades
They take out a full-page ad in the
    trades to announce their arrival
And Mary Lou she found out how to
    cope, she rides to heaven on a
    gyroscope
The *Daily News* asks her for the dope
She says "Man the dope's that there's
    still hope"

Señorita, Spanish rose, wipes her eyes
    and blows her nose
Uptown in Harlem she throws a rose to
    some lucky young matador

lost in the flood

The ragamuffin gunner is returnin'
  home like a hungry runaway
He walks through town all alone
"He must be from the fort" he hears the
  high school girls say
His countryside's burnin' with wolfman
  fairies dressed in drag for homicide
The hit-and-run plead sanctuary, 'neath
  a holy stone they hide
They're breakin' beams and crosses
  with a spastic's reelin' perfection
Nuns run bald through Vatican halls
  pregnant, pleadin' Immaculate
  Conception
And everybody's wrecked on Main Street
  from drinking unholy blood
Sticker smiles sweet as Gunner
  breathes deep, his ankles caked
  in mud
And I said "Hey Gunner man, that's
  quicksand, that's quicksand, that
  ain't mud
Have you thrown your senses to the war
  or did you lose them in the flood?"

That pure American brother dull-eyed
  and empty-faced

Races Sundays in Jersey in a Chevy
  stock super eight
He rides 'er low on the hip, on the side
  he's got "bound for glory" in red,
  white and blue flash paint
He leans on the hood telling racing
  stories, the kids call him Jimmy the
  Saint
Well that blaze and noise boy, he's
  gunnin' that bitch loaded to blastin'
  point
He rides head first into a hurricane and
  disappears into a point
And there's nothin' left but some blood
  where the body fell
That is, nothin' left that you could sell
Just junk all across the horizon, a real
  highwayman's farewell
And I said "Hey kid, you think that's oil?
  Man, that ain't oil, that's blood"
I wonder what he was thinking when he
  hit that storm
Or was he just lost in the flood?

Eighth Avenue sailors in satin shirts
  whisper in the air

Some storefront incarnation of Maria,
  she's puttin' on me the stare
And Bronx's best apostle stands with
  his hand on his own hardware
Everything stops, you hear five quick
  shots, the cops come up for air
And now the whiz-bang gang from
  uptown, they're shootin' up the street
And that cat from the Bronx starts
  lettin' loose
But he gets blown right off his feet
And some kid comes blastin' 'round the
  corner but a cop puts him right away
He lays on the street holding his leg
  screaming something in Spanish
Still breathing when I walked away
And someone said "Hey man, did you
  see that? His body hit the street with
  such a beautiful thud"
I wonder what the dude was sayin', or
  was he just lost in the flood?
Hey man, did you see that, those poor
  cats are sure messed up
I wonder what they were gettin' into, or
  were they all just lost in the flood?

the
angel

The angel rides with hunchbacked
   children, poison oozing from his
   engine
Wieldin' love as a lethal weapon on his
   way to hubcap heaven
Baseball cards poked in his spokes, his
   boots in oil he's patiently soaked
The roadside attendant nervously jokes
   as the angel's tires stroke his
   precious pavement

The interstate's choked with nomadic
   hordes
In Volkswagen vans with full running
   boards dragging great anchors
Followin' dead-end signs into the stores
The angel rides by humpin' his hunk
   metal whore

Madison Avenue's claim to fame in a
   trainer bra with eyes like rain
She rubs against the weather-beaten
   frame and asks the angel for his
   name
Off in the distance the marble dome
Reflects across the flatlands with a
   naked feel off into parts unknown
The woman strokes his polished chrome
   and lies beside the angel's bones

for you

Princess cards she sends me with her
regards
Barroom eyes shine vacancy, to see her
you got to look hard
Wounded deep in battle, I stand stuffed
like some soldier undaunted
To her Cheshire smile, I'll stand on file,
she's all I ever wanted
But you let your blue walls get in the
way of these facts
Honey get your carpetbaggers off my
back
You wouldn't even give me time to cover
my tracks
You said "Here's your mirror and your
ball and jacks" but they're not what I
came for and I'm sure you see that
too
I came for you, for you, I came for you,
but you did not need my urgency
I came for you, for you, I came for you,
but your life was one long emergency
And your cloud line urges me and my
electric surges free
Crawl into my ambulance, your pulse is
getting weak
Reveal yourself all now to me girl while
you've got the strength to speak
'Cause they're waiting for you at
Bellevue with their oxygen masks
But I could give it all to you now if only
you could ask

And don't call for your surgeon, even he
says it's too late
It's not your lungs this time, it's your
heart that holds your fate
Don't give me my money honey I don't
want it back
You and your pony face and your union
jack
Well take your local joker and teach him
how to act
I swear I was never that way even when
I really cracked
Didn't you think I knew that you were
born with the power of a locomotive
Able to leap tall buildings in a single
bound
And your Chelsea suicide with no
apparent motive
You could laugh and cry in a single
sound

And your strength is devastating in the
face of all these odds
Remember how I kept you waiting when
it was my turn to be the god

You were not quite half so proud when I
found you broken on the beach
Remember how I poured salt on your
tongue and hung just out of reach
And the band they played the homecoming theme as I caressed your
cheek
That ragged jagged melody she still
clings to me like a leech
But that medal you wore on your chest
always got in the way
Like a little girl with a trophy so soft to
buy her way
We were both hitchhikers but you had
your ear tuned to the roar
Of some metal-tempered engine on an
alien distant shore
So you left to find a better reason than
the one we were living for
And it's not that nursery mouth I came
back for
And it's not the way you're stretched out
on the floor
'Cause I've broken all your windows and
I've rammed through all your doors
And who am I to ask you to lick my
sores
And you should know that's true
I came for you, for you, I came for you,
but you did not need my urgency
I came for you, for you, I came for you,
but your life was one long emergency
And your cloud line urges me and my
electric surges free

spirit in the night

Crazy Janey and her mission man were
   back in the alley tradin' hands
'Long came Wild Billy with his friend
   G-man all duded up for Saturday
   night
Well Billy slammed on his coaster
   brakes and said anybody wanna go
   up to Greasy Lake
It's about a mile down on the dark side
   of Route 88
I got a bottle of rosé so let's try it
We'll pick up Hazy Davy and Killer Joe
   and I'll take you all out to where the
   gypsy angels go
They're built like light
And they dance like spirits in the night
   (all night) in the night (all night)
Oh you don't know what they can do
   to you
Spirits in the night (all night) in the
   night (all night)
Stand right up now and let them shoot
   through you

Well now Wild Billy was a crazy cat and
   he shook some dust out of his coon-
   skin cap
He said "Trust some of this it'll show
   you where you're at or at least it'll
   help you really feel it"
By the time we made it up to Greasy
   Lake I had my head out the window
   and Janey's fingers were in the cake
I think I really dug her 'cause I was too
   loose to fake

I said "I'm hurt," she said "Honey let
   me heal it"
And we danced all night to a soul fairy
   band
And she kissed me just right like only a
   lonely angel can
She felt so nice, just as soft as a spirit
   in the night (all night) in the night
   (all night)
Janey don't know what she do to you
Like a spirit in the night (all night) in
   the night (all night)
Stand right up and let it shoot through
   me

Now the night was bright and the stars
   threw light on Billy and Davy dancin'
   in the moonlight
They were down near the water in a
   stoned mud fight
Killer Joe gone passed out on the lawn
Well now Hazy Davy got really hurt, he
   ran into the lake in just his socks
   and a shirt
Me and Crazy Janey was makin' love in
   the dirt singin' our birthday songs
Janey said it was time to go so we
   closed our eyes and said good-bye to
   gypsy angel row, felt so right
Together we moved like spirits in the
   night (all night) in the night (all
   night)

it's hard to be a saint in the city

I had skin like leather and the
diamond-hard look of a cobra
I was born blue and weathered but I
burst just like a supernova
I could walk like Brando right into
the sun
Then dance just like a Casanova
With my blackjack and jacket and hair
slicked sweet
Silver star studs on my duds just like a
Harley in heat
When I strut down the street I could feel
its heartbeat
The sisters fell back and said "Don't
that man look pretty"
The cripple on the corner cried out
"Nickels for your pity"
Them gasoline boys downtown sure talk
gritty
It's so hard to be a saint in the city

I was the king of the alley, mama I
could talk some trash
I was the prince of the paupers crowned
downtown at the beggar's bash
I was the pimp's main prophet, I kept
everything cool
Just a backstreet gambler with the luck
to lose
And when the heat came down and it
was left on the ground
The devil appeared like Jesus through
the steam in the street
Showin' me a hand I knew even the
cops couldn't beat
I felt his hot breath on my neck as I
dove into the heat
It's so hard to be a saint when you're
just a boy out on the street

And the sages of the subway sit just
like the living dead

As the tracks clack out the rhythm,
their eyes fixed straight ahead
They ride the line of balance and hold
on by just a thread
But it's too hot in these tunnels, you
can get hit up by the heat
You get up to get out at your next stop
but they push you back down in
your seat
Your heart starts beatin' faster as you
struggle to your feet
Then you're out of that hole and back
up on the street

And them Southside sisters sure look
pretty
The cripple on the corner cries out
"Nickels for your pity"
And them downtown boys sure talk
gritty
It's so hard to be a saint in the city

the wild, the innocent & the e street shuffle

With the original E Street Band in West End, New Jersey *(clockwise)*: David Sancious, Vini Lopez, Garry Tallent, Danny Federici, Clarence Clemons

eading into *The Wild, the Innocent*, I was intent on taking control of the recording process. *Greetings* was primarily an acoustic record with a rhythm section. That was fine for the first time out, but I had made my living primarily as a rock musician. Now I wanted to continue the lyrical content of my first album but add to it the physicality my music always had coming up through the clubs. For this record, I was determined to call on my songwriting ability and my bar band experience.

By now, my producers, Mike Appel and Jim Cretecos, had a chance to see me perform with a band. They saw that I knew what I was doing, and now I was determined to take the reins and go in the creative direction I wanted.

The opening cut, "The E Street Shuffle," is a reflection of a community that was partly imagined and partly real. It was the early '70s: blues, R&B, and soul were still heavily influential and heard often along the Jersey Shore. Musically, I based the song on Major Lance's '60s hit "Monkey Time," a dance song. The cast of characters came vaguely from Asbury Park at the turn of the decade. I wanted to describe a neighborhood, a way of life, and I wanted to invent a dance with no exact steps. It was just the dance you did every day and every night to get by.

I'd lived in Asbury Park for the past three years. I watched the town suffer some pretty serious race rioting and slowly begin to close down. The Upstage club, where I met most of the members of the E Street Band, had shut its doors. The boardwalk was still operating, but the crowds were sparse. Many of the usual summer vacationers were now passing Asbury Park by for less troubled locations farther south along the coast.

I'd been evicted from my apartment above the beauty salon, so I moved on myself and was living with my girlfriend in a garage apartment, five minutes from Asbury, in Bradley Beach. This is where I wrote "4th of July, Asbury Park (Sandy)," a goodbye to my adopted hometown and the life I'd lived there before I recorded. Sandy was a composite of some of the girls I'd known along the Shore. I used the boardwalk and the closing down of the town as a metaphor for the end of a summer romance and the changes I was experiencing in my own life.

"Kitty's Back" was a remnant of some of the jazz-tinged rock I occasionally played with a few of my earlier bands. It was a swing tune, a shuffle, a distorted piece of big band music. In '74 I had to have songs that could capture audiences that had no idea who I was. As an opening act, I didn't have much time to make an impact. I wrote several wild, long pieces—"Thunder Crack,"

With Mike Appel in the studio

"Kitty's Back," "Rosalita"—that were arranged to leave the band and the audience exhausted and gasping for breath. Just when you thought the song was over, you'd be surprised by another section, taking the music higher. It was, in spirit, what I'd taken from the finales of the great soul revues. When you left the stage after performing one of these, you'd worked to be remembered.

"Wild Billy's Circus Story" was a black comedy based on my memories of the fairs and the Clyde Beatty/Cole Bros. Circus that visited Freehold every summer when I was a kid. They'd set up a midway and pitch their tents in a field across from the racetrack not far from my house. It was also a song about the seduction and loneliness of a life outside the margins of everyday life. At twenty-four, already having spent a good deal of time on the road, for better or worse, that was the life I wanted to live.

"Incident on 57th Street" and "New York City Serenade" were my romantic stories of New York City, a place that had been my getaway from small-town New Jersey since I was sixteen. "Incident" particularly featured a theme I'd return to often in the future: the search for redemption. Over the next twenty years I'd work this one like only a good Catholic boy could.

"Rosalita" was my musical autobiography. It was my "getting out of town" preview for *Born to Run,* with more humor. I wrote it as a kiss-off to everybody who counted you out, put you down, or decided you weren't good enough. The lyrics also took a peek into the future—"Someday we'll look

With David Sancious

back on this and it will all seem funny." Not that it would all BE funny, but that it would all SEEM

funny. Probably one of the most useful lines I've ever written.

At the time of *The Wild, the Innocent,* I had no success, so I had no real concerns about where

I was going. I was going up, I hoped, or at least out. With a record contract and a touring band, I

was better off than most of my friends. They were either jobless or locked down into the nine-to-

five. I felt lucky to be doing what I loved most.

With the opening chords of "Rosie," I geared up my band and hit the road without dread. That

would come later.

the e street shuffle

Sparks fly on E Street when the boy
    prophets walk it handsome and hot
All the little girls' souls go weak when
    the man-child gives them a double
    shot
Them schoolboy pops pull out all the
    stops on a Friday night
The teenage tramps in skintight pants
    do the E Street dance and every-
    thing's all right
Well the kids down there are either
    dancing or hooked up in a scuffle
Dressed in snakeskin suits packed with
    Detroit muscle
They're doin' the E Street shuffle
Now those E Street brats in twilight
    duel flash like phantoms in full star
    stream
Down fire trails on silver nights with
    blonde girls pledged sweet sixteen
The newsboys say the heat's been bad
    since Power Thirteen gave a trooper
    all he had in summer scuffle
And Power's girl, Little Angel, been on
    the corner keepin' those crazy boys
    out of trouble
Little Angel steps the shuffle like she
    ain't got no brains

She's death in combat down on Lover's
    Lane
She drives all them local boys insane
Little Angel says "Oh, oh, everybody
    form a line
Oh, oh, everybody form a line"
Sparks light on E Street when the boy
    prophets walk it handsome and hot
All them little girls' souls go weak when
    the man-child gives them a double
    shot
Little Angel hangs out at Easy Joe's, it's
    a club where all the riot squad goes
    when they're cashin' in for a cheap
    hustle
But them boys are still on the corner
    loose and doin' that lazy E Street
    shuffle
As them sweet summer nights turn into
    summer dreams
Little Angel picks up Power and he slips
    on his jeans
And they move on out down to the
    scene
All the kids are dancin'

Opposite: At the Main Point in Philadelphia

E Street Shuffle

~~Sparks~~ ~~fly~~ Sparks fly!

~~The lights are bright~~ on E street when

(street) the boy prophets walk it handsome +

hot

the little girls souls go weak when the

man child gives'em a double shot

those schoolboy pops pull out all the

stops on friday night

those Teenage Tramps in skin tight

pants do the E street dance and it's

all right (the

~~those~~ ~~some~~ ~~kids~~ ~~down~~ ~~there~~

~~when~~ ~~they~~ ~~...~~

~~...~~

rainbow/radio ~~with~~ ~~...~~

rondeau/torpedo

zero/volcano ~~seiker~~ ~~the~~ ~~e~~ ~~street~~ ~~shuffle~~

gigolo/rider

those E street babes in ...

~~the~~ slip ... like ~~the~~ phantoms

full

down through the scene (in slow stream)

chance (M. how) ~~down~~ ~~...~~ ~~...~~

plugged   met

slo (promised) golden girl ...   Tools

6-man

Power 13 + Angelo ... you know they

E.C. slo   on the E.Z. Buffalo + hooks him in a hustle

it was somewhere down in Jobongo they picked up

these E street brats in twilight
dual flash like phantoms in full
   Dorstream
down fire trails on silver nights
  with blonde girls sweet 16 *Pledged*
the mens boys say she heals
been bad since power 13 gave
a trooper all he had in late summer
  scuffle
powers girl little angel been
  on the corner keeping those
crazy boys out of trouble

little angel can step the shuffle
like she ain't got no brain power
says she's death in combat
  down on lovers lane she drives
all the boys insane

little angel says
  come on down
  towlove the (cause the)

4th of july, asbury park [sandy]

Sandy, the fireworks are hailin' over
Little Eden tonight
Forcin' a light into all those stoney
faces left stranded on this warm July
Down in town the circuit's full with
switchblade lovers so fast, so shiny,
so sharp
As the wizards play down on Pinball
Way on the boardwalk way past dark
And the boys from the casino dance
with their shirts open like Latin
lovers on the shore
Chasin' all them silly New York virgins
by the score

Sandy, the aurora is risin' behind us
This pier lights our carnival life
forever
Love me tonight for I may never see you
again
Hey Sandy girl, my baby

Now the greasers they tramp the streets
or get busted for sleeping on the
beach all night
Them boys in their high heels, ah
Sandy, their skins are so white
And me I just got tired of hangin' in
them dusty arcades bangin' them
pleasure machines
Chasin' the factory girls underneath the
boardwalk where they promise to
unsnap their jeans
And you know that tilt-a-whirl down on
the south beach drag
I got on it last night and my shirt got
caught
And they kept me spinnin'
I didn't think I'd ever get off

Oh Sandy, the aurora is risin' behind us
This pier lights our carnival life on the
water
Runnin', laughin' 'neath the boardwalk
with the boss's daughter
I remember, Sandy girl, now baby

Sandy, that waitress I was seeing lost
her desire for me
I spoke with her last night, she said
she won't set herself on fire for me
anymore
She worked that joint under the boardwalk, she was always the girl you
saw boppin' down the beach with the
radio
The kids say last night she was dressed
like a star in one of them cheap little
seaside bars and I saw her parked
with Loverboy out on the Kokomo
Did you hear the cops finally busted
Madam Marie for tellin' fortunes
better than they do
For me this boardwalk life is through
You ought to quit this scene too

Sandy, the aurora is rising behind us
This pier lights our carnival life
forever
Oh love me tonight and I promise I'll
love you forever

kitty's back

Catlong sighs holding Kitty's black
  tooth
She left to marry some top cat, ain't it
  the cold truth
And there hasn't been a tally since
  Sally left the alley
Since Kitty left with Big Pretty things
  have got pretty thin
It's tight on this fence since them
  young dudes are musclin' in

Jack Knife cries 'cause baby's in a
  bundle
She goes running nightly, lightly
  through the jungle
And them tin cans are explodin' out in
  the ninety-degree heat
Cat somehow lost his baby down on
  Bleecker Street
It's sad but it sure is true
Cat shrugs his shoulders, sits back and
  sighs
Ooh, what can I do, ooh, what can I do?
Ooh, what can I do, ooh, what can I do?

Catlong lies back bent on a trash can
Flashing lights cut the night, dude in
  white says he's the man

Well you better learn to move fast when
  you're young or you're not long
  around
Cat somehow lost his Kitty down in the
  city pound
So get right, get tight, get down
Well who's that down at the end of the
  alley?
She's been gone so long

Kitty's back in town, here she comes
  now
Kitty's back in town
Kitty's back in town, here she comes
  now
Kitty's back in town
Kitty's back in town, here she comes
  now
Kitty's back in town

Now Cat knows his Kitty's been untrue
And that she left him for a city dude
But she's so soft, she's so blue
When he looks into her eyes
He just sits back and sighs
Ooh, what can I do, ooh, what can I do?

wild billy's circus story

The machinist climbs his ferris wheel
    like a brave
And the fire eater's lyin' in a pool of
    sweat, victim of the heatwave
Behind the tent the hired hand tightens
    his legs on the sword swallower's
    blade
And circus town's on the shortwave

The runway lies ahead like a great false
    dawn
Fat lady, big mama, Missy Bimbo sits
    in her chair and yawns
And the man-beast lies in his cage
    sniffin' popcorn
As the midget licks his fingers and
    suffers Missy Bimbo's scorn
Circus town's been born

Whoa, and a press roll drummer go
    ballerina to and fro
Cartwheelin' up on that tightrope with
    a cannon blast lightnin' flash
Movin' fast through the tent Mars bent,
    he's gonna miss his fall
Oh God save the human cannonball
And the flying Zambinis watch
    Margarita do her neck twist
And the ringmaster gets the crowd to
    count along: "Ninety-five, ninety-six,
    ninety-seven"
A ragged suitcase in his hand, he

steals silently away from the circus
    grounds
And the highway's haunted by the
    carnival sounds
They dance like a great greasepaint
    ghost on the wind
A man in baggy pants, a lonely face, a
    crazy grin
Runnin' home to some small Ohio town
Jesus send some good women to save
    all your clowns

And circus boy dances like a monkey on
    barbed wire
And the barker romances with a junkie,
    she's got a flat tire
And now the elephants dance real funky
    and the band plays like a jungle fire
Circus town's on the live wire
And the strong man Sampson lifts the
    midget Little Tiny Tim way up on his
    shoulders, way up
And carries him on down the midway
    past the kids, past the sailors
To his dimly lit trailer
And the ferris wheel turns and turns
    like it ain't ever gonna stop
And the circus boss leans over,
    whispers in the little boy's ear "Hey
    son, you wanna try the big top?"
All aboard, Nebraska's our next stop

incident on 57th street

Spanish Johnny drove in from the
underworld last night
With bruised arms and broken rhythm
in a beat-up old Buick
But dressed just like dynamite
He tried sellin' his heart to the hard
girls over on Easy Street
But they sighed "Johnny it falls apart
so easy and you know hearts these
days are cheap"
And the pimps swung their axes and
said "Johnny you're a cheater"
Well the pimps swung their axes and
said "Johnny you're a liar"
And from out of the shadows came
a young girl's voice said "Johnny
don't cry"
Puerto Rican Jane, oh won't you tell me
what's your name
I want to drive you down to the other
side of town where paradise ain't so
crowded, there'll be action goin'
down on Shanty Lane tonight
All them golden-heeled fairies in a real
bitch fight
Pull .38s and kiss the girls good night
Oh good night, it's all right Jane
Now let them black boys in to light the
soul flame

We may find it out on the street tonight
baby
Or we may walk until the daylight
maybe

Well like a cool Romeo he made his
moves, oh she looked so fine
Like a late Juliet she knew he'd never
be true but then she didn't really
mind
Upstairs a band was playin', the singer
was singin' something about goin'
home
She whispered "Spanish Johnny, you
can leave me tonight but just don't
leave me alone"

And Johnny cried "Puerto Rican Jane,
word is down the cops have found
the vein"
Oh them barefoot boys they left their
homes for the woods
Them little barefoot street boys they
say homes ain't no good
They left the corners, threw away all
their switchblade knives and kissed
each other good-bye

Johnny was sittin' on the fire escape

watchin' the kids playin' down the
street
He called down "Hey little heroes,
summer's long but I guess it ain't
very sweet around here anymore"
Janey sleeps in sheets damp with
sweat, Johnny sits up alone and
watches her dream on, dream on
And the sister prays for lost souls, then
breaks down in the chapel after
everyone's gone

Jane moves over to share her pillow but
opens her eyes to see Johnny up and
puttin' his clothes on
She says "Those romantic young boys
All they ever want to do is fight"
Those romantic young boys
They're callin' through the window
"Hey Spanish Johnny, you want to make
a little easy money tonight?"
And Johnny whispered:
Good night, it's all tight Jane
I'll meet you tomorrow night on Lover's
Lane
We may find it out on the street tonight
baby
Or we may walk until the daylight
maybe

rosalita
[come out tonight]

Spread out now Rosie, doctor come cut
loose her mama's reins
You know playin' blindman's bluff is a
little baby's game
You pick up Little Dynamite, I'm gonna
pick up Little Gun
And together we're gonna go out
tonight and make that highway run
You don't have to call me lieutenant
Rosie and I don't want to be your son
The only lover I'm ever gonna need's
your soft sweet little girl's tongue
Rosie you're the one
Dynamite's in the belfry playin' with the
bats
Little Gun's downtown in front of
Woolworth's tryin' out his attitude on
all the cats
Papa's on the corner waitin' for the bus
Mama she's home in the window waitin'
up for us
She'll be there in that chair when they
wrestle her upstairs
'Cause you know we ain't gonna come
I ain't here on business
I'm only here for fun
And Rosie you're the one

CHORUS:
Rosalita jump a little lighter
Señorita come sit by my fire

I just want to be your love, ain't no lie
Rosalita you're my stone desire

Jack the Rabbit and Weak Knees Willie,
you know they're gonna be there
Ah, Sloppy Sue and Big Bones Billy,
they'll be comin' up for air
We're gonna play some pool, skip some
school, act real cool
Stay out all night, it's gonna feel all
right
So Rosie come out tonight, baby come
out tonight
Windows are for cheaters, chimneys for
the poor
Closets are for hangers, winners use
the door
So use it, Rosie, that's what it's there
for

(CHORUS)

Now I know your mama she don't like
me 'cause I play in a rock and roll
band
And I know your daddy he don't dig me
but he never did understand
Papa lowered the boom, he locked you
in your room
I'm comin' to lend a hand
I'm comin' to liberate you, confiscate

you, I want to be your man
Someday we'll look back on this and it
will all seem funny
But now you're sad, your mama's mad
And your papa says he knows that I
don't have any money
Tell him this is his last chance to get
his daughter in a fine romance
Because the record company, Rosie,
just gave me a big advance

My tires were slashed and I almost
crashed but the Lord had mercy
My machine she's a dud, I'm stuck in
the mud somewhere in the swamps
of Jersey
Hold on tight, stay up all night 'cause
Rosie I'm comin' on strong
By the time we meet the morning light I
will hold you in my arms
I know a pretty little place in Southern
California down San Diego way
There's a little café where they play
guitars all night and all day
You can hear them in the back room
strummin'
So hold tight baby 'cause don't you
know daddy's comin'

(CHORUS)

new york city serenade

Billy he's down by the railroad track
Sittin' low in the backseat of his
  Cadillac
Diamond Jackie, she's so intact
As she falls so softly beneath him
Jackie's heels are stacked
Billy's got cleats on his boots
Together they're gonna boogaloo down
  Broadway and come back home with
  the loot
It's midnight in Manhattan, this is no
  time to get cute
It's a mad dog's promenade
So walk tall or baby don't walk at all

Fish lady, oh fish lady
She baits them tenement walls
She won't take corner boys
They ain't got no money
And they're so easy
I said "Hey, baby
Won't you take my hand
Walk with me down Broadway
Well mama take my arm and move with
  me down Broadway"
I'm a young man, I talk it real loud
Yeah babe I walk it real proud for you
Ah, so shake it away
So shake away your street life
Shake away your city life
Hook up to the train
And hook up to the night train
Hook it up

Hook up to the train
But I know she won't take the train, no
  she won't take the train
Oh she won't take the train, no she
  won't take the train
Oh she won't take the train, no she
  won't take the train
Oh she won't take the train, no she
  won't take the train
She's afraid them tracks are gonna slow
  her down
And when she turns this boy'll be gone
So long, sometimes you just gotta
  walk on, walk on

Hey vibes man, hey jazz man, play me
  your serenade
Any deeper blue and you'd be playin' in
  your grave
Save your notes, don't spend 'em on the
  blues boy
Save your notes, don't spend 'em on
  the darlin' yearling sharp boy
Straight for the church note ringin',
  vibes man sting a trash can
Listen to your junk man
Listen to your junk man
Listen to your junk man
He's singin', he's singin', he's singin'
All dressed up in satin, walkin' down
  the alley
He's singin', singin', singin', singin'

born to run

n 1974, though struggling through the aftermath of the riots and economic depression, Asbury Park still managed to come to life on Friday and Saturday nights. Down by the boardwalk, Kingsley and Ocean avenues formed a sort of racetrack oval that locals called the Circuit. It surrounded all the bars and nightclubs, including the Stone Pony, the new hub of the city's rock music scene.

In '70s New Jersey, the car was still a powerful image. That summer I bought my first set of wheels for two thousand dollars. It was a '57 Chevy with dual, four-barrel carbs, a Hurst on the floor, and orange flames spread across the hood. I was living in a small house in West Long Branch, up the coast from Asbury. I had a record player by the side of my bed. At night I'd lie back and listen to records by Roy Orbison, the Ronettes, the Beach Boys, and other great '60s artists. These were records whose full depth I'd missed the first time around. But now I was appreciating their craft and power.

One day I was playing my guitar on the edge of my bed, working on some song ideas, and the words "born to run" came into my head. At first I thought it was the name of a movie or something I'd seen on a car spinning around the Circuit, but I couldn't be certain. I liked the phrase because it suggested a cinematic drama I thought would work with the music I was hearing in my head.

Before we had a chance to record it, "Born to Run" developed as a song that the E Street Band and I played live on the road. That gave me an opportunity to feel out the arrangement. But live, the limitations of a seven-piece band were never going to provide me with the range of sound I needed to realize the song's potential. It was the first piece of music I wrote and conceived as a studio production. It was connected to the long, live pieces I'd written previously by the twists and turns of the arrangement.

But "Born to Run" was more condensed; it maintained the excitement of "Rosalita" while delivering its message in less time and with a shorter burst of energy. This was a turning point, and it allowed me to open up my music to a far larger audience. "Born to Run" was a long time coming; it took me six months to write. But it proved to be the key to my songwriting for the rest of the record. Lyrically, I was entrenched in classic rock and roll images, and I wanted to find a way to use those images without their feeling anachronistic.

Born to Run was released into post-Vietnam America. There was a coming gas crisis . . . no gas . . . no cars. People were contemplating a country that was finite, where resources and life had lim-

The Jabongans (a.k.a. the E Street Band) with new members Max Weinberg *(third from right)* and Roy Bittan *(far right)*

With Jon Landau

its. Slowly, the dread that I managed to keep out of "Rosalita" squeezed its way into the lives of the people on *Born to Run.*

It was during this time that I began my friendship with Jon Landau, a Boston music writer. I sent him a tape of *Born to Run* while he was in the hospital recuperating from an illness. He later moved to New York City. There we struck up a relationship—hanging out, talking music, and listening to records. When I ran into trouble recording the rest of the album, he stepped in and helped me get the job done. We moved into the Record Plant in New York City and hired Jimmy Iovine to engineer. We stripped down the songs and streamlined the arrangements. We developed a more direct sound with cleaner lines.

"Thunder Road" opens the album, introducing its characters and its central proposition: Do you want to take a chance? On us? On life? You're then led through the band bio and block party of "Tenth Avenue Freeze-out," the broken friendships of "Backstreets," out into the open with "Born to Run," and into the dark city and spiritual battleground of "Jungleland."

Few of the album's songs were written on guitar. The orchestral sound of *Born to Run* came from most of the songs being written on piano. It was on the keyboard that I could find the arrangements needed to accompany the stories I was writing. "Born to Run," which began on the guitar with the riff that opens the song, was finished on the piano.

The characters on *Born to Run* were less eccentric and less local than on *Greetings* and *The Wild, the Innocent.* They could have been anybody and everybody. When the screen door slams on "Thunder Road," you're not necessarily on the Jersey Shore anymore. You could be anywhere in America. These were the beginnings of the characters whose lives I would trace in my work for the next two decades.

As a songwriter I always felt one of my jobs was to face the questions that evolve out of my music and search for the answers as best as I could. For me, the primary questions I'd be writing about for the rest of my work life first took form in the songs on *Born to Run* ("I want to know if love is real."). It was the album where I left behind my adolescent definitions of love and freedom.

Born to Run was the dividing line.

thunder road

The screen door slams
Mary's dress waves
Like a vision she dances across the
   porch
As the radio plays
Roy Orbison singing for the lonely
Hey that's me and I want you only
Don't turn me home again
I just can't face myself alone again
Don't run back inside
Darling you know just what I'm here for
So you're scared and you're thinking
That maybe we ain't that young any-
   more
Show a little faith, there's magic in the
   night
You ain't a beauty but hey you're all
   right
Oh and that's all right with me

You can hide 'neath your covers
And study your pain
Make crosses from your lovers
Throw roses in the rain
Waste your summers praying in vain
For a savior to rise from these streets

Well now I'm no hero
That's understood
All the redemption I can offer, girl
Is beneath this dirty hood
With a chance to make it good some-
   how
Hey what else can we do now
Except roll down the window
And let the wind blow back your hair
Well the night's busting open
These two lanes will take us anywhere
We got one last chance to make it real
To trade in these wings on some wheels
Climb in back, heaven's waiting on
   down the tracks
Oh come take my hand
We're riding out tonight to case the
   promised land
Oh Thunder Road, oh Thunder Road
Oh Thunder Road
Lying out there like a killer in the sun
Hey I know it's late, we can make it if
   we run
Oh Thunder Road, sit tight, take hold
Thunder Road

Well I got this guitar
And learned how to make it talk
And my car's out back
If you're ready to take that long walk
From your front porch to my front seat
The door's open but the ride ain't free
And I know you're lonely
For words that I ain't spoken
But tonight we'll be free
All the promises'll be broken
There were ghosts in the eyes
Of all the boys you sent away
They haunt this dusty beach road
In the skeleton frames of burned-out
   Chevrolets
They scream your name at night in the
   street
Your graduation gown lies in rags at
   their feet
And in the lonely cool before dawn
You hear their engines roaring on
But when you get to the porch they're
   gone on the wind
So Mary climb in
It's a town full of losers
And I'm pulling out of here to win

tenth avenue freeze-out

Teardrops on the city
Bad Scooter searching for his groove
Seem like the whole world walking
  pretty
And you can't find the room to move
Well everybody better move over, that's
  all
'Cause I'm running on the bad side
And I got my back to the wall
Tenth Avenue freeze-out
Tenth Avenue freeze-out

Well I was stranded in the jungle
Trying to take in all the heat they was
  giving
The night is dark but the sidewalk's
  bright
And lined with the light of the living
From a tenement window a transistor
  blasts

Turn around the corner things got real
  quiet real fast
I walked into a Tenth Avenue freeze-out
Tenth Avenue freeze-out
And I'm all alone, I'm all alone
And kid you better get the picture
And I'm on my own, I'm on my own
And I can't go home

When the change was made uptown
And the Big Man joined the band
From the coastline to the city
All the little pretties raise their hands
I'm gonna sit back right easy and
  laugh
When Scooter and the Big Man bust
  this city in half
With the Tenth Avenue freeze-out
Tenth Avenue freeze-out

n i g h t

You get up every morning at the sound
  of the bell
You get to work late and the boss
  man's giving you hell
Till you're out on a midnight run
Losing your heart to a beautiful one
And it feels right
As you lock up the house
Turn up the lights
And step out into the night

And the world is busting at its seams
And you're just a prisoner of your
  dreams
Holding on for your life
'Cause you work all day
To blow 'em away in the night

The rat traps filled with soul crusaders
The circuits lined and jammed with
  chromed invaders
And she's so pretty that you're lost in
  the stars
As you jockey your way through the cars

And sit at the light as it changes to
  green
With your faith in your machine
Off you scream into the night

And you're in love with all the wonder it
  brings
And every muscle in your body sings
As the highway ignites
You work nine to five
And somehow you survive
Till the night
Hell all day they're busting you up on
  the outside
But tonight you're gonna break on
  through to the inside
And it'll be right, it'll be right
And it'll be tonight

And you know she will be waiting there
And you'll find her somehow you swear
Somewhere tonight
You run sad and free
Until all you can see is the night

backstreets

One soft infested summer
Me and Terry became friends
Trying in vain to breathe
The fire we was born in
Catching rides to the outskirts
Tying faith between our teeth
Sleeping in that old abandoned beach
   house
Getting wasted in the heat
And hiding on the backstreets
Hiding on the backstreets
With a love so hard and filled with
   defeat
Running for our lives at night on them
   backstreets

Slow dancing in the dark
On the beach at Stockton's Wing
Where desperate lovers park
We sat with the last of the Duke Street
   Kings
Huddled in our cars

Waiting for the bells that ring
In the damp heat of the night we could
   let loose of everything
To go running on the backstreets
Running on the backstreets
Terry you swore we'd live forever
Taking it on them backstreets together

Endless juke joints and Valentine drag
Where dancers scraped the tears
Up off the street dressed down in rags
Running into the darkness
Some hurt bad, some really dying
At night sometimes it seemed
You could hear the whole damn city
   crying
Blame it on the lies that killed us
Blame it on the truth that ran us down
You can blame it all on me, Terry
It don't matter to me now
When the breakdown hit at midnight
There was nothing left to say

But I hated him
And I hated you when you went away

Laying here in the dark
You're like an angel on my chest
Just another tramp of hearts
Crying tears of faithlessness
Remember all the movies, Terry
We'd go see
Trying to learn how to walk like the
   heroes
We thought we had to be
And after all this time
To find we're just like all the rest
Stranded in the park
And forced to confess
To hiding on the backstreets
Hiding on the backstreets
Where we swore forever friends
On the backstreets until the end
Hiding on the backstreets
Hiding on the backstreets

"...like a newsboy hat ... but bigger ..."

born to run

In the day we sweat it out on the
   streets of a runaway American dream
At night we ride through mansions of
   glory in suicide machines
Sprung from cages on Highway 9
Chrome-wheeled fuel-injected
And steppin' out over the line
Baby this town rips the bones from your
   back
It's a death trap, it's a suicide rap
We gotta get out while we're young
'Cause tramps like us, baby we were
   born to run

Wendy let me in, I wanna be your friend
I want to guard your dreams and
   visions
Just wrap your legs 'round these velvet
   rims
And strap your hands across my
   engines

Together we could break this trap
We'll run till we drop, baby we'll never
   go back
Will you walk with me out on the wire
'Cause baby I'm just a scared and
   lonely rider
But I gotta know how it feels
I want to know if your love is wild
Girl I want to know if love is real

Beyond the Palace hemipowered drones
   scream down the boulevard
The girls comb their hair in rearview
   mirrors
And the boys try to look so hard
The amusement park rises bold and
   stark
Kids are huddled on the beach in the
   mist
I wanna die with you out on the streets
   tonight

In an everlasting kiss

The highway's jammed with broken
   heroes
On a last chance power drive
Everybody's out on the run tonight
But there's no place left to hide
Together, Wendy, we can live with the
   sadness
I'll love you with all the madness in my
   soul
Someday girl, I don't know when, we're
   gonna get to that place
Where we really want to go
And we'll walk in the sun
But till then tramps like us
Baby we were born to run

she's the one

With her killer graces
And her secret places
That no boy can fill
With her hands on her hips
Oh and that smile on her lips
Because she knows that it kills me
With her soft French cream
Standing in that doorway like a dream
I wish she'd just leave me alone
Because French cream won't soften
    them boots
And French kisses will not break that
    heart of stone
With her long hair falling
And her eyes that shine like a midnight
    sun
Oh she's the one
She's the one

That thunder in your heart
At night when you're kneeling in the
    dark
It says you're never gonna leave her
But there's this angel in her eyes
That tells such desperate lies

And all you want to do is believe her
And tonight you'll try
Just one more time
To leave it all behind
And to break on through
Oh she can take you
But if she wants to break you
She's gonna find out that ain't so easy
    to do
And no matter where you sleep
Tonight or how far you run
Oh she's the one
She's the one

Oh and just one kiss
She'd fill them long summer nights
With her tenderness
That secret pact you made
Back when her love could save you
From the bitterness
Oh she's the one
Oh she's the one
Oh she's the one
Oh she's the one

meeting across the river

Hey Eddie, can you lend me a few bucks
And tonight can you get us a ride?
Gotta make it through the tunnel
Got a meeting with a man on the other
    side

Hey Eddie, this guy he's the real thing
So if you want to come along
You gotta promise you won't say
    anything
'Cause this guy don't dance
And the word's been passed this is our
    last chance

We gotta stay cool tonight, Eddie
'Cause man, we got ourselves out on
    that line
And if we blow this one
They ain't gonna be looking for just me
    this time
And all we gotta do is hold up our end

Here stuff this in your pocket
It'll look like you're carrying a friend
And remember, just don't smile
Change your shirt 'cause tonight we
    got style

Well Cherry says she's gonna walk
'Cause she found out I took her radio
    and hocked it
But Eddie, man, she don't understand
That two grand's practically sitting here
    in my pocket
And tonight's gonna be everything that
    I said
And when I walk through that door
I'm just gonna throw that money on the
    bed
She'll see this time I wasn't just talking
Then I'm gonna go out walking

Hey Eddie, can you catch us a ride?

Worksheet for "Meeting Across the River"

Hey Eddie can you lend me a few bucks
    And tonight can you get us a ride
gotta make it through the tunnel I gotta
    meetin' with a man on the other side
And Eddie this guys he's the real
thing so if you wanna come along
    you gotta promise you won't say anything
cause this guy don't dance ~~and don't~~
~~you know this is ear~~ the words passed
            this our last chance

We gotta stay
        ~~too~~ cool tonight Eddie man we got
ourselves the rep on the line
            blow lose
    And if we ~~~~ this one they ain't
gonna be looking for just me this time
    Al we gotta do is hold up our end
here stuff this in your pocket it'll look
like your carryin a freind remember
    don't smile change your shirt tonight
were gotta ~~is~~ style

    Cherry says she's gonna walk cause
I took the radio and hocked it
but man she don't understand that
two grands practically in my pocket
tonight so gonna be everything I
said and when I walk through
that door I'm gonna throw that
money on the bed she'll see this time
I wasn't just talkin then I'm gonna
    go out walkin

Following a seventy-two-hour studio marathon, *Born to Run* was completed. At 8:30 A.M. the band rehearsed to begin the tour in Providence, Rhode Island, that night.

jungleland

The Rangers had a homecoming
In Harlem late last night
And the Magic Rat drove his sleek
    machine
Over the Jersey state line
Barefoot girl sitting on the hood of a
    Dodge
Drinking warm beer in the soft summer
    rain
The Rat pulls into town, rolls up his
    pants
Together they take a stab at romance
And disappear down Flamingo Lane

Well the Maximum Lawmen run down
    Flamingo
Chasing the Rat and the barefoot girl
And the kids 'round there live just like
    shadows
Always quiet, holding hands
From the churches to the jails
Tonight all is silence in the world
As we take our stand
Down in Jungleland

The midnight gang's assembled
And picked a rendezvous for the night
They'll meet 'neath that giant Exxon
    sign

That brings this fair city light
Man there's an opera out on the
    turnpike
There's a ballet being fought out in
    the alley
Until the local cops
Cherry tops
Rips this holy night
The street's alive
As secret debts are paid
Contacts made, they vanish unseen
Kids flash guitars just like switch-
    blades
Hustling for the record machine
The hungry and the hunted
Explode into rock and roll bands
That face off against each other out in
    the street
Down in Jungleland

In the parking lot the visionaries
Dress in the latest rage
Inside the backstreet girls are dancing
To the records that the DJ plays
Lonely-hearted lovers
Struggle in dark corners
Desperate as the night moves on
Just one look and a whisper
And they're gone

Beneath the city two hearts beat
Soul engines running through a night
    so tender
In a bedroom locked
In whispers of soft refusal
And then surrender
In the tunnels uptown
The Rat's own dream guns him down
As shots echo down them hallways in
    the night
No one watches when the ambulance
    pulls away
Or as the girl shuts out the bedroom
    light

Outside the street's on fire
In a real death waltz
Between what's flesh and what's
    fantasy
And the poets down here
Don't write nothing at all
They just stand back and let it all be
And in the quick of a knife
They reach for their moment
And try to make an honest stand
But they wind up wounded
Not even dead
Tonight in Jungleland

darkness on the edge of town

fter *Born to Run* I wanted to write about life in the close confines of the

small towns I grew up in. In 1977 I was living on a farm in Holmdel, New

Jersey. It was there that I wrote most of the songs for *Darkness on the Edge*

of Town.

I was twenty-seven and the product of Top 40 radio. Songs like the

Animals' "It's My Life" and "We Gotta Get Out of This Place" were infused with an early pop class

consciousness. That, along with my own experience—the stress and tension of my father's and

mother's life that came with the difficulties of trying to make ends meet—influenced my writing.

I had a reaction to my own good fortune. I asked myself new questions. I felt a sense of account-

ability to the people I'd grown up alongside of. I began to wonder how to address that feeling. Also, at that time, I was in a battle with my former manager for the rights and control of my music. I stood the chance of losing much of what I had worked for and accomplished. All of this led to the turn my writing took on *Darkness*.

I began to listen seriously to country music around this time. I discovered Hank Williams. I liked the fact that country dealt with adult topics, and I wanted to write songs that would resonate down the road. Film, always important to my writing, became an even greater influence on this album. I always liked the flash and outlaws of B pictures—Robert Mitchum in *Thunder Road* and Arthur Ripley's *Gun Crazy*. I'd recently seen John Ford's *The Grapes of Wrath* for the first time. I sought out '40s and '50s film noir such as Jacques Tourneur's *Out of the Past*. It was the feeling of men and women struggling against a world closing in that drew me to those films. Even the title, *Darkness on the Edge of Town,* owed a lot to American noir.

Musically I wanted the record to sound leaner and less grand than *Born to Run.* That sound wouldn't suit these songs or the people I was now writing about. Chuck Plotkin, an LA record man, came in near the end of the album and helped us get a tighter, more modern mix. He helped us focus the songs in a way we'd been unable to and allowed us to bring the record to completion. There was a lot of variation in the material we recorded, but I edited out anything I thought broke the album's tension. After *Born to Run,* I wanted to ensure that my music continued to have value and a sense of place.

The songs were difficult to write. I remember spending hours trying to come up with a single verse. "Badlands," "Prove It All Night," and "Promised Land" all had a chorus but few lyrics. I was searching for a tone somewhere between *Born to Run*'s spiritual hopefulness and '70s cynicism. I

With Chuck Plotkin, Jon Landau, and engineer Jimmy Iovine

wanted my new characters to feel weathered, older, but not beaten. The sense of daily struggle in each song greatly increased. The possibility of transcendence or any sort of personal redemption felt a lot harder to come by. This was the tone I wanted to sustain. I intentionally steered away from any hint of escapism and set my characters down in the middle of a community under siege. Weeks, even months went by, before I had something that felt right.

The songs came together slowly, line by line, piece by piece. The titles were big: "Adam Raised a Cain," "Darkness on the Edge of Town," "Racing in the Street." "Adam Raised a Cain" used biblical images to summon up the love and bitterness between a father and son. "Darkness on the Edge of Town" dealt with the idea that the setting for personal transformation is often found at the end of your rope. In "Racing in the Street" I wanted my street racers to carry the years between the car songs of the '60s and 1978 America. To make "Racing" and those other big titles personal, I had to infuse the music with my own hopes and fears. If you don't do that, your characters ring hollow, and you're left with rhetoric, words without meaning.

Most of my writing is emotionally autobiographical. You've got pull up the things that mean something to you in order for them to mean anything to your audience. That's how they know you're not kidding.

With the record's final verse, "Tonight I'll be on that hill . . . ," my characters stand unsure of their fate, but dug in and committed. By the end of *Darkness* I'd found my adult voice.

Along time ago we chose to ride or live

Hot Rod Storys
The Hot Rod Story
Breakers Point
Breakout
The Wait

Prove it All Night

I Believe in a Promised Land

Fury / Let the Quiet Rain Fall

Initiations / The Ride

Thunder Road /

Kingsley Avenue

The Searchers
The
Workin
The Taker
Collision /
Factory / Tarn

Titles

2 - try brighter start
3 - best
4 - good
5 - say out loud

Angels on Wheels / American Relay
Demolition Derby   Hot Rod Angels
Speed Racing through America (In)
Racin in the Street / Buried Crosses
Medals
Speed Racing In America
Ride the Serpent / Grace / National
Daytona Screamer
Ramrod / Kansas City Confidential
Street Racer
Ramrodin
Faded Medals
Dirt Tracker
Badlands
Daytona
Gun Crazy / Bear Town
Who Walk in Darkness   Ignition
Monroe County Line / Go
Waynesboro County   Something in the Night

Often I'd work from pages of titles I collected
as I went along.

badlands

Lights out tonight
Trouble in the heartland
Got a head-on collision
Smashin' in my guts, man
I'm caught in a crossfire
That I don't understand
But there's one thing I know for sure,
   girl
I don't give a damn
For the same old played out scenes
I don't give a damn
For just the in-betweens
Honey, I want the heart, I want the soul
I want control right now
You better listen to me, baby
Talk about a dream
Try to make it real
You wake up in the night
With a fear so real
You spend your life waiting
For a moment that just won't come
Well don't waste your time waiting

CHORUS:
Badlands, you gotta live it every day
Let the broken hearts stand
As the price you've gotta pay
We'll keep pushin' till it's understood
And these badlands start treating us
   good

Workin' in the fields
Till you get your back burned
Workin' 'neath the wheel
Till you get your facts learned
Baby, I got my facts
Learned real good right now
You better get it straight, darlin'
Poor man wanna be rich
Rich man wanna be king
And a king ain't satisfied
Till he rules everything
I wanna go out tonight
I wanna find out what I got

I believe in the love that you gave me
I believe in the faith that can save me
I believe in the hope and I pray
That someday it may raise me
Above these badlands

(CHORUS)

For the ones who had a notion
A notion deep inside
That it ain't no sin to be glad you're
   alive
I wanna find one face that ain't looking
   through me
I wanna find one place
I wanna spit in the face of these
   badlands

(CHORUS)

adam raised a cain

In the summer that I was baptized
My father held me to his side
As they put me to the water
He said how on that day I cried
We were prisoners of love, a love in
    chains
He was standin' in the door, I was
    standin' in the rain
With the same hot blood burning in our
    veins
Adam raised a Cain

All of the old faces
Ask you why you're back
They fit you with position
And the keys to your daddy's Cadillac
In the darkness of your room
Your mother calls you by your true name
You remember the faces, the places,
    the names

You know it's never over, it's relentless
    as the rain
Adam raised a Cain

In the Bible Cain slew Abel
And east of Eden he was cast
You're born into this life paying
For the sins of somebody else's past
Daddy worked his whole life for nothing
    but the pain
Now he walks these empty rooms
    looking for something to blame
You inherit the sins, you inherit the
    flames
Adam raised a Cain
Lost but not forgotten
From the dark heart of a dream
Adam raised a Cain

something in the night

I'm riding down Kingsley
Figuring I'll get a drink
Turn the radio up loud
So I don't have to think
I take her to the floor
Looking for a moment when the world
   seems right
And I tear into the guts
Of something in the night

You're born with nothing
And better off that way
Soon as you've got something
They send someone to try and take it
   away
You can ride this road till dawn
Without another human being in sight
Just kids wasted on
Something in the night

Nothing is forgotten or forgiven
When it's your last time around
I got stuff running 'round my head
That I just can't live down

When we found the things we loved
They were crushed and dying in the dirt
We tried to pick up the pieces
And get away without getting hurt
But they caught us at the state line
And burned our cars in one last fight
And left us running burned and blind
Chasing something in the night

candy's room

In Candy's room there are pictures of
    her heroes on the wall
But to get to Candy's room you gotta
    walk the darkness of Candy's hall
Strangers from the city call my baby's
    number and they bring her toys
When I come knocking she smiles pretty
She knows I wanna be Candy's boy
There's a sadness hidden in that pretty
    face
A sadness all her own from which no
    man can keep Candy safe

We kiss, my heart's pumpin' to my brain
The blood rushes in my veins when I
    touch Candy's lips
We go driving, driving deep into the
    night
I go driving deep into the light in
    Candy's eyes

She says baby if you wanna be wild

You got a lot to learn, close your eyes
Let them melt, let them fire
Let them burn
'Cause in the darkness there'll be
    hidden worlds that shine
When I hold Candy close she makes the
    hidden worlds mine

She has fancy clothes and diamond
    rings
She has men who give her anything she
    wants but they don't see
That what she wants is me

Oh and I want her so
I'll never let her go, no no no
She knows that I'd give
All that I've got to give
All that I want, all that I live
To make Candy mine
Tonight

New Fast Song (Candy)

In Candys room sh has pictures of her saviour / hang
          on the wall but to get to Candys room
you gotta walk Candys hall
          so rangers fran sh city call my babys number
they bring her toys but when I come knokn sh
          smiles prettly she knows that im gonna be Candys
              boy

there   somewhere in the darkness   I find   hidden worlds
    (so strange new worlds)   that shine through the (Anger)
fear   bravences   mist

          Then
+ when we kiss my hearts comes pushin / slamin through
              my skin   for a moment she begs me in
      that wheel slow moanin   thats when the sadnres begins
    I get visions (glimpses) (dreams) of avenging angels of eden
          with their white horse + flaming swords
              can blow this whole town into the sea
but they cant touch Candy + me
          our love they cannot destroy
I will forever be Candys boy

          she says baby if you wanna be wild you gotta
          get   some things   you got a lot to learn
          you gotta let   your (wings) heart burn
          so come with me   together (we) baby well drive all
well go drivin together into the night
          through the heart of a fire fight into no rain

we go drivin south   that spider off the line + then we kiss

          from a world well meet / burn / take / know
without end

racing in the street

I got a '69 Chevy with a 396
Fuelie heads and a Hurst on the floor
She's waiting tonight down in the
    parking lot
Outside the 7-11 store
Me and my partner Sonny built her
    straight out of scratch
And he rides with me from town to town
We only run for the money, got no
    strings attached
We shut 'em up and then we shut 'em
    down

Tonight, tonight the strip's just right
I wanna blow 'em off in my first heat
Summer's here and the time is right
For racin' in the street

We take all the action we can meet
And we cover all the northeast states
When the strip shuts down we run 'em
    in the street

From the fire roads to the interstate
Some guys they just give up living
And start dying little by little, piece by
    piece
Some guys come home from work and
    wash up
And go racin' in the street

Tonight, tonight the strip's just right
I wanna blow 'em all out of their seats
Calling out around the world, we're
    going racin' in the street

I met her on the strip three years ago
In a Camaro with this dude from L.A.
I blew that Camaro off my back
And drove that little girl away
But now there's wrinkles around my
    baby's eyes
And she cries herself to sleep at night
When I come home the house is dark

She sighs "Baby did you make it all
    right?"
She sits on the porch of her daddy's
    house
But all her pretty dreams are torn
She stares off alone into the night
With the eyes of one who hates for just
    being born
For all the shut-down strangers and
    hot-rod angels
Rumbling through this promised land
Tonight my baby and me we're gonna
    ride to the sea
And wash these sins off our hands

Tonight, tonight the highway's bright
Out of our way mister you best keep
'Cause summer's here and the time is
    right
For racin' in the street

the promised land

On a rattlesnake speedway in the Utah
    desert
I pick up my money and head back into
    town
Driving 'cross the Waynesboro county
    line
I got the radio on and I'm just killing
    time
Working all day in my daddy's garage
Driving all night chasing some mirage
Pretty soon, little girl, I'm gonna take
    charge

CHORUS:
The dogs on Main Street howl
'Cause they understand
If I could take one moment into my
    hands
Mister, I ain't a boy, no I'm a man
And I believe in a promised land

I've done my best to live the right way
I get up every morning and go to work
    each day
But your eyes go blind and your blood
    runs cold

Sometimes I feel so weak I just want to
    explode
Explode and tear this whole town apart
Take a knife and cut this pain from my
    heart
Find somebody itching for something to
    start

(CHORUS)

There's a dark cloud rising from the
    desert floor
I packed my bags and I'm heading
    straight into the storm
Gonna be a twister to blow everything
    down
That ain't got the faith to stand its
    ground
Blow away the dreams that tear you
    apart
Blow away the dreams that break your
    heart
Blow away the lies that leave you noth-
    ing but lost and brokenhearted

(CHORUS)

factory

Early in the morning factory whistle
  blows
Man rises from bed and puts on his
  clothes
Man takes his lunch, walks out in the
  morning light
It's the working, the working, just the
  working life

Through the mansions of fear, through
  the mansions of pain
I see my daddy walking through the
  factory gates in the rain
Factory takes his hearing, factory gives
  him life
The working, the working, just the
  working life

End of the day, factory whistle cries
Men walk through these gates with
  death in their eyes
And you just better believe, boy
Somebody's gonna get hurt tonight
It's the working, the working, just the
  working life

streets
of fire

When the night's quiet and you don't
    care anymore
And your eyes are tired and there's
    someone at your door
And you realize you wanna let go
And the weak lies and the cold walls
    you embrace
Eat at your insides and leave you face
    to face with
Streets of fire

I'm wandering, a loser down these
    tracks
I'm dying but girl I can't go back
'Cause in the darkness I hear somebody
    call my name
And when you realize how they tricked
    you this time
And it's all lies but I'm strung out on
    the wire
In these streets of fire

I live now only with strangers
I talk to only strangers
I walk with angels that have no place
Streets of fire

prove it all night

I've been working real hard trying to get
my hands clean
Tonight we'll drive that dusty road from
Monroe to Angeline
To buy you a gold ring and pretty dress
of blue
Baby, just one kiss will get these things
for you
A kiss to seal our fate tonight
A kiss to prove it all night
Prove it all night
Girl, there's nothing else that we can do
So prove it all night, prove it all night
And girl I'll prove it all night for you

Everybody's got a hunger, a hunger they
can't resist
There's so much that you want, you
deserve much more than this
But if dreams came true oh wouldn't
that be nice
But this ain't no dream we're living
through tonight

Girl, you want it, you take it, you pay
the price
To prove it all night, prove it all night
Prove it all night, babe, and call the
bluff
Prove it all night, prove it all night
Girl, I prove it all night for your love

Baby, tie your hair back in a long white
bow
Meet me in the fields out behind the
dynamo
You hear the voices telling you not to go
They made their choices and they'll
never know
What it means to steal, to cheat, to lie
What it's like to live and die
To prove it all night, prove it all night
Girl, there's nothing else that we can do
So prove it all night, prove it all night
And girl I'll prove it all night for you

Prove It All Night

An baby me + you Ain't one just alikey
yea baby me + you we both save ours for the
little criminals night
do you really think these streets will Allow you
your paradise
An honey if dreams came true baby would'nt that
be nice
you wan't it you Take it you better be ready
to pay the price

same 2nd verse

2 lane road black op on 61 / flat strip of blacktop
2 old cowboys open our foot run
cross 500 feet of blacktop headlights fade to fade
I swing open the door den baby it's so quiet
we let the engines roar As we dissolve into tonight if feels so nice
but somethen starts screamin   flash our lights
+ somethen

drers / you know I'll give my best
or is these a dream we
this ain't no dream were moving through tonight

baby wants a mustang / stallion

you look so wild tonight   stole been cheated lied

how much you hurt for the ones who stole who cheated
who lied to prove it
baby you can just give it up nothen a word

The evolution of "Prove It All Night" beginning with a few lines from the second verse

prove it all night + don't let nothin slide
+ girl 2nd prove it all night baby at yor side

dark sky up ahead + I gud nothin left below
It's all gud gore dead + baby, I gud don't know

dark sky up ahead + I don't feel nothin here below
It's all gore dead - the same old misfit row /road/
                    for on down on
                Prove it
drivin into ~~Monroe~~ + I ain't gonna sleep tonight
gotta find my little frend holdin steady at the traffic light
                                            bout steady
I swing open th door you hop in by my side
we let the engine roar blow off everything in sight
but somethin keeps pushin inside pushin to prove it...

so whisper in my ear the pretty things you want
don't + let the night play with yor fears (but) baby don't let
            yourself get caught
caught on the inside cause there you can't exist
baby we could ride (roam) me I'm gonna ride these out tonite
gust searchin (lookin) for a kiss to seal (out) my fate
Tonite a kiss to prove it allnight
            + don't let nothin slide (come girl you can let)
prove it all nite at yor side

baby needs a cadillac baby needs a dress of blue
+ honey if I can I'll get these things for you
gust give me your love blind me like the sun
then maybe me + you we could be like the ones
who stole who cheated who lied who lived + died to prove...

I need your love to blind me like the sun
then may be me + you girl we could be like the
        ones who stole who cheated who lied
who lived + died (died + lived to prove it all night)

(Chorus)
I prove all night for love
  "   "   "   "   or die
prove it all night girl until we hit
  "   "   "   "   or quit
  "   "   "   "   for you
                                        die
+ Ain't this just a dream were movin through
   Tonight a dream where you want it you take it
        you better
                                    before the end of the night want
you can whisper in my ear the pretty things you need / see
    sleep tight + don't fear   by the dawn

    I lane road block out on 88 2 sets of
    cross a flat strip of blacktop her dlights far off here

    [whisper the pretty things you want then then he
          dark
    the night plays with your fears / hold on tight
        Come close little girl cause we won't stop
                        tonight
    whisper in my ear the pretty things you'd like

    ain't this just a dream

    the dark plays with your fears + we won't sleep tonight
    whisper in my ear + we won't sleep tonight

    whisper in my ear the things you want

Prove it

young thing/little girl on the corner lookin for a freind
young blood   wanna have a freind
baby cuss shoot your line + well take it
(to) till the end
I swing open the door you hop in by my
          side   take
we let the engine roar we make it till it's
          right   until we blow off the night
but somethin keeps pushin me inside   pushin to...
          (chorus)

poss 3rd v.   theres a darkness up ahead + I'm empty scared
out here   down below (through + through)
It's all just the radios gone dead + girl I don't know
     dead   where we can go (I don't know what
(what were gonna do I don't know)   were gonna do)
I don't stop baby I can't (don't) (knowhow) to stop
               got a hunger I can't resist
          I'm lookin for True, real (real true) love
          I'm lookin for a kiss to (that will) seal my
          (our) fate tonight a kiss to ...

▦

poss 2. v.   my baby (little girl) wants a cadillac she
                wants a dress of blue
          honey (baby) if I could I'd get those things for
                can
                you
          if dreams came true an baby wouldn't that
                be nice
          this ain't no dream were movin through
                tonight
                                          magic
          you ain't no dream + baby I ain't no toy
          you want it you take it (got it) you better
          be ready to pay the price to prove...

Tomba...

Prove it

baby tie your hair back in a long white
            bow
meet me in the fields out behind the dynamo
hold me close promise you'll never let me go
we'll burn it all then baby we'll let go
we'll throw it all on one last ride

promise you won't quit promise you'll never let go
baby let 'em fall cause girl they'll never know
                                      know an
what it's like to throw it all on one last ride
+ push to prove it...

A kiss to seal the promise we made to night

baby tie your hair back in a long white bow
                    night   couply oustirls of
meet me in the fields out behind the dynamo monroe
                            Telling   for
you hear their voices calling you not to go
                                              glad to stay home ago
but girl they made their choices + they'll never know
                          fight fett
what it's like to know for just one moment what it's
          got it   live
like you got it right + push to prove it...   ride
to fight for the right to feel like your alive + push

the choice is yours you got the right but just be ready to...

were drawn till the hit you can use the backseat
      for a bed
nobody out here gives a damn whether your alive or dead
                            folks   fear
oh yea we can ride thru our baby what a tear
      folks in town
cause nobody don't give a damn what goes on
              here
on out there they'll never gonna reach drive into the
heart for the fight

The third verse emerges.

Prove it (New)

Baby I'll buy you a cadillac and a pretty dress
                        of blue
baby, I'll do my very best to get these things for
(if dreams....)   *I got my own kind of hunger
      that I can't resist   you got so much that
I want
ridin dust roads from Monroe into Angeline
me + Willy ford pullin into Angeline / Caroline
Willy lets the engines roar nose runnin on borrowed time
I got my

doubleshifts won't quit
I work 2 jobs till I got my hands clean
            joinin into
then we'll ride these dust roads from Monroe to Angeline
+ I'll buy you a cadillac (and a ring) + a pretty dress of blue
sweet thing for jus one kiss (I'll swear I'd got)
    I'll got...   A kiss to seal...

Everybody's got their own hunger   somethin they can't resist
I got my own hunger   I can't resist
these so much baby me + you better more   than this
                      we deserve (so much)
if dreams...

* I'll buy you a cadillac +   a pretty blue dress
I swear I'll get these things for you for jus one kiss...

Everybodys got their own hunger   somethin they can't resist
these plent that I want these so much that I were
                                     missed
oh and if dreams come true wouldn't that..

baby we been trapped on the inside before we're on bay
cause baby out on the outside we ain't nobodys but who

I/

Ⓐ I've worked 18 jobs till I got my hands clean
we're gonna ride the dirt roads from Monroe to Angeline
'case I got a hunger a hunger I can't resist
there's so much that I want girl right now I want
a kiss to seal...

Ⓑ baby wants a cadilac she wants a dress of blue
                    ring of gold
+ honey if I can I get these things for you
if dreams came true Ann nothin' that be nice
but it ain't no dream were livin through tonight
you want it you take it you ~~better be a~~ pay the price

Ⓒ so baby tie your hair back in a long white bow
meet me in the fields out behind the dynamo
can we been trapped on the inside before
            we even begun
c'mon
well break out to the outside we can be just
    like the ones who sold who cheated who
    lied (who chose their side's stood + tried + died
        took their chances + lived + died

II/

Ⓐ Baby I've worked 2 jobs, girl to get my hands clean
tonight we drive these dust roads out to Angeline
+ I'll buy you a ~~gold~~ gold ring + a pretty dress of blue
for just one kiss I'll get these things for you
a kiss

Ⓑ they I got a hunger a hunger I can't resist
there's so much that I want too much
        that I've just missed
if dreams came true oh...

Different versions of the verses moving toward the final

Prove it

~~I been tryin to get my hands clean~~
~~Tonight well~~

I been workin real hard tryin to get my
                    hands clean
Tonight well drive that dusty road all
        on into
        the way of Angeline
(Tonight well drive that dusty road from Monroe)
    to Angeline

I'll buy you a gold ring + a pretty dress
            of blue
And baby just one kiss will get these
            things for you
A kiss to seal our fate tonight
    A kiss to prove it all night

theres nothin else that we can do
and girl I prove it all night for you
we all got our own
Everybodys got a hunger a hunger they can't resist
   and girl
You say theres so much that you want say you
        deserve much more than this
Well honey if dreams came true Anna
            wouldnt that be nice
but girl this aint no dream were livin
        here through tonight
this aint no paradise
you want it you take it you pay
        the price to (you)

Prove it all night girl and call the bluff
    I prove it all night for your love

Prove it

baby tie your hair back in a long white
                    bow
+ meet me in the fields out behind
                    the dynamo
you hear the(ir) voices telling you not to go
well ~~girl~~ baby they made their choices and
        + girl they'll never know
what it ~~means~~ like to steal to cheat to lie
How it   what it's ~~like~~ means to live + die to prove
feels   it all night

(~~babe~~ we don't let nothin slide
 & prove it all baby at your side)

prove it all night baby just for you

KODAK SAFETY FILM 6075

KODAK SAFETY FILM 6075

KODAK SAFETY FILM 6075

darkness on the edge of town

They're still racing out at the trestles
But that blood it never burned in her
   veins
Now I hear she's got a house up in
   Fairview
And a style she's trying to maintain
Well if she wants to see me
You can tell her that I'm easily found
Tell her there's a spot out 'neath
   Abram's Bridge
And tell her there's a darkness on the
   edge of town

Everybody's got a secret, sonny
Something that they just can't face
Some folks spend their whole lives
   trying to keep it
They carry it with them every step that
   they take
Till someday they just cut it loose

Cut it loose or let it drag 'em down
Where no one asks any questions
Or looks too long in your face
In the darkness on the edge of town

Some folks are born into a good life
Other folks get it anyway anyhow
I lost my money and I lost my wife
Them things don't seem to matter
   much to me now
Tonight I'll be on that hill 'cause I can't
   stop
I'll be on that hill with everything I got
Lives on the line where dreams are
   found and lost
I'll be there on time and I'll pay the cost
For wanting things that can only be
   found
In the darkness on the edge of town

the ties that bind

sherry darling

jackson cage

two hearts

independence day

hungry heart

out in the street

crush on you

you can look (but you better not touch)

i wanna marry you

the river

point blank

cadillac ranch

i'm a rocker

fade away

stolen car

ramrod

the price you pay

drive all night

wreck on the highway

the river

he sound and song content of *The River* was both a reaction to and an extension of the ideas explored on *Darkness on the Edge of Town. Darkness* had been a modern, technically produced studio album, less eccentric sounding and more conventionally recorded than *Born to Run.* On *The River* I knew I wanted more of the roughness and spontaneity of our live show. I was concerned about moving too close to the sterility of '70s record production. Steve Van Zandt, my old friend and guitarist, had joined the production team, which included Jon Landau and Chuck Plotkin. As veterans of the local New Jersey club scene, Steve and I enjoyed a strong, close relationship. Now together, we began to steer the recording of *The River* in a rawer direction.

This was the album where the E Street Band really came into its own in the studio. We struck the right balance between a garage band and the professionalism required to make good records. Plus, I had a clear idea of what I wanted to hear. I wanted the snare drum to explode and I wanted less separation between the instruments. Also, after the seriousness of *Darkness,* I wanted to give myself a lot more flexibility with the emotional range of the songs I chose. Our shows had always been filled with fun and I didn't want to see that left out this time around.

The first song we cut for *The River* was "Roulette," which I'd written on the tail of the Three Mile Island nuclear accident. It had an appropriately paranoid lyric and an exciting track, but it never made it to the record. Next, we cut "The Ties That Bind," with the band playing in a wood-paneled studio with open mikes over the drumkit to get that live resonance. Everything was splashing around. We weren't in complete control of the way everything sounded, but that was the idea.

Minus—at the moment—any grand strategy, I was just trying to write some good songs. If anything, I wanted to create songs that would sound good played by a bar band. To me, that was basically what we remained. All the years I'd been performing, I'd often start the show with something that sounded like it came out of the garage. In the past, these were the kinds of songs that fell by the wayside when we went into the studio to record. For *The River,* I wanted to make sure this part of what I did wouldn't get lost.

After some recording we prepared a single album and handed it in to the record company. When I listened to it later on, I felt that it just wasn't good enough. The songs lacked the kind of unity and conceptual intensity I liked my music to have. So we went back into the studio and another year went by. Many songs were cut, and many were judged not up to par. Part of the problem might have been the less meticulous, more instinctive way that I approached songwriting this

time around. Once you have a few successful records under your belt, you become more aware of people's expectations. You can become too cautious. On *The River* I was determined to let the band play live and let the music happen. Some nights it worked, and some nights it didn't. It was in struggling to reconcile my previous and present recording approaches that the album found its identity. We decided to make *The River* a double record. I'd try for the best of both worlds: more pop songs in a looser conceptual framework.

The River got its emotional depth from its ballads. "Point Blank," "Independence Day," "The River," "Stolen Car" were all song-stories. "Stolen Car" was the predecessor for a good deal of the music I'd be writing in the future. It was inner-directed, psychological; this was the character whose progress I'd soon be following on *Tunnel of Love.* He was the archetype for the male role in my later songs about men and women.

The album got its energy from "Cadillac Ranch," "Hungry Heart," "Two Hearts," "Ramrod," and the other club rockers. This was the music I wrote to provide fuel for our live show and to create a counterbalance to the ballads that began showing up more and more in my work. These songs provided an emotional release and an external point of view before the ballads returned you to the internal lives of the characters.

The River also was my first attempt to write about the commitments of home and marriage. Country music, once again, continued to be important. One night in my hotel room in New York, I started singing Hank Williams's "My Bucket's Got a Hole In It." I drove back to New Jersey that night and sat up in my room writing "The River." I used a narrative folk voice—just a guy in a bar telling his story to the stranger on the next stool. I based the song on the crash of the construction industry in late '70s New Jersey and the hard times that fell on my sister and her family. I watched my brother-in-law lose his good-paying job and work hard to survive without complaint. When my sister first heard it, she came backstage, gave me a hug, and said, "That's my life." That song crystallized my concerns and was a style of writing I'd develop in greater depth and detail on *Nebraska* and *The Ghost of Tom Joad.*

The album closes with a title stolen from a Roy Acuff song. "Wreck on the Highway" is about confronting one's own death and stepping into the adult world where time is finite. On a rainy highway the character witnesses a fatal accident. He drives home, and lying awake that night next to his lover, he realizes that you have a limited number of opportunities to love someone, to do your work, to be a part of something, to parent your children, to do something good.

the ties that bind

You been hurt and you're all cried out
you say
You walk down the street pushing
people outta your way
You packed your bags and all alone you
wanna ride
You don't want nothin', don't need no
one by your side
You're walkin' tough, baby but you're
walkin' blind
To the ties that bind
The ties that bind
Now you can't break the ties that bind

Cheap romance it's all just a crutch

You don't want nothin' that anybody
can touch
You're so afraid of being somebody's
fool
Not walkin' tough, baby not walkin' cool
You walk cool but darlin' can you walk
the line
And face the ties that bind
The ties that bind
Now you can't break the ties that bind

I would rather feel the hurt inside
Yes I would darlin'
Than know the emptiness your heart
must hide
Yes I would darlin', yes I would darlin'

Yes I would baby

You sit and wonder just who's gonna
stop the rain
Who'll ease the sadness, who's gonna
quiet the pain
It's a long dark highway and a thin
white line
Connecting, baby, your heart to mine
We're runnin' now but darlin' we will
stand in time
To face the ties that bind
The ties that bind
Now you can't break the ties that bind
You can't forsake the ties that bind

sherry darling

Your mama's yappin' in the backseat
Tell her to push over and move them
    big feet
Every Monday morning I gotta drive her
    down to the unemployment agency
Well this morning I ain't fighting, tell
    her I give up
Tell her she wins if she'll just shut up
But it's the last time that she's gonna
    be riding with me

CHORUS:
You can tell her there's a hot sun beat-
    ing on the blacktop
She keeps talkin' she'll be walkin' that
    last block
She can take a subway back to the
    ghetto tonight
Well I got some beer and the highway's
    free
And I got you and baby you got me
Hey, hey, hey, what you say, Sherry
    darling

Well there's girls meltin' out on the
    beach
And they're so fine but so out of reach
'Cause I'm stuck in traffic down on
    Fifty-third Street
Now Sherry, my love for you is real
But I didn't count on this package deal
And baby, this car just ain't big enough
    for her and me

(CHORUS)

Well let there be sunlight, let there be
    rain
Let the brokenhearted love again
Sherry, we can run with our arms open
    wide before the tide
To all the girls down at Sacred Heart
And all you operators back in the park
Say hey, hey, hey, what you say, Sherry
    darling
Say hey, hey, what you say, Sherry
    darling

jackson cage

Driving home she grabs something
  to eat
Turns a corner and drives down the
  street
Into a row of houses she just melts
  away
Like the scenery in another man's play
Into a house where the blinds are
  closed
To keep from seeing things she don't
  wanna know
She pulls the blinds and looks out on
  the street
The cool of the night takes the edge off
  the heat
In the Jackson Cage
Down in the Jackson Cage
You can try with all your might
But you're reminded every night
That you been judged and handed life
Down in the Jackson Cage

Every day ends in wasted motion
Just crossed swords on the killing floor
To settle back is to settle without
  knowing
The hard edge that you're settling for
Because there's always just one more
  day
And it's always gonna be that way

Little girl, you've been down here so
  long
I can tell by the way that you move you
  belong to
The Jackson Cage
Down in Jackson Cage
And it don't matter just what you say
Are you tough enough to play the game
  they play
Or will you just do your time and fade
  away
Down into the Jackson Cage

Baby there's nights when I dream of a
  better world
But I wake up so downhearted, girl
I see you feeling so tired and confused
I wonder what it's worth to me or you
Just waiting to see some sun
Never knowing if that day will ever
  come
Left alone standing out on the street
Till you become the hand that turns the
  key down in
Jackson Cage
Down in Jackson Cage
Well darlin', can you understand
The way that they will turn a man
Into a stranger to waste away
Down in the Jackson Cage

Your mammas yappin in the backseat
        babe can't you tell her to shudup
Every monday mornin I gotta drag her
        to the agency   all down to
tell   skydout cut plead to her case
tell her this mornin I aint fightin
" "   she wins baby I give up
" "   It's her last ride in the machine wait
        + see

tell her there's a hot sun beatin on the blacktop
    if she keep talkin she'll be walkin that
        last block
tell her she can take a taxi back to the
    ghetto cause I aint comin back

        beer
I got some wine + the highways free I got you
    + babe you got me   cherry darlin
                              girl
                           Darlene
there's a hot sun beatin on the blacktop
    no matter what gets down baby I can't stop
    the music's playin + it wont stop

(I been thrown out on my own with a heart half-broken
        + my radio's blown
    no matter how she trys to shut up

So your mammas yappin in the backseat
    let's open the door + kick her out on the street
        hey hey, what ya say Debby May

Cherry darling? Darlene? Debby May? Decisions, decisions, decisions . . .

bright

so let there be sunlight let there be rain
let there be broken hearts and let them love again
let the broken hearted love again

there are girls melting on the beach from works boys like me
they won't give a damn of reach from workin boys like us

light

let us run before the tide with our hearts
open wide let 'em all come runnin
& man's take it all in

and let the keeper of the secret heart and all
back the park
you operators down in Dreams park
know that she's bad and trouble you this time
when you have to you let go roll up the
windows turn the radio loud
and you're loved the music comin from the romance
the radio just a buzz in the background

Tell her she don't stop pleadin that case
I'm gonna turn up this radio till I blast
that grin off her face
don't look

two hearts

I went out walking the other day
Seen a little girl crying along the way
She'd been hurt so bad said she'd
    never love again
Someday your crying, girl, will end
And you'll find once again

CHORUS:
Two hearts are better than one
Two hearts, girl, get the job done
Two hearts are better than one

Once I spent my time playing tough guy
    scenes
But I was living in a world of childish
    dreams
Someday these childish dreams must
    end
To become a man and grow up to
    dream again

Now I believe in the end

(CHORUS)

Sometimes it might seem like it was
    planned
For you to roam empty hearted through
    this land
Though the world turns you hard and
    cold
There's one thing, mister, that I know
That's if you think your heart is stone
And that you're rough enough to whip
    this world alone
Alone, buddy, there ain't no peace of
    mind
That's why I'll keep searching till I find
My special one

(CHORUS)

independence day

Well Papa go to bed now, it's getting
  late
Nothing we can say is gonna change
  anything now
I'll be leaving in the morning from Saint
  Mary's Gate
We wouldn't change this thing even if
  we could somehow
'Cause the darkness of this house has
  got the best of us
There's a darkness in this town that's
  got us too
But they can't touch me now
And you can't touch me now
They ain't gonna do to me
What I watched them do to you

So say good-bye, it's Independence Day
It's Independence Day
All down the line
Just say good-bye, it's Independence
  Day
It's Independence Day this time

Now I don't know what it always was
  with us
We chose the words, and yeah, we drew
  the lines
There was just no way this house could
  hold the two of us
I guess that we were just too much of
  the same kind

Well say good-bye, it's Independence
  Day
It's Independence Day, all boys must
  run away
So say good-bye, it's Independence Day
All men must make their way come
  Independence Day

Now the rooms are all empty down at
  Frankie's joint
And the highway she's deserted clear
  down to Breaker's Point
There's a lot of people leaving town

now, leaving their friends, their
  homes
At night they walk that dark and dusty
  highway all alone

Well Papa go to bed now, it's getting
  late
Nothing we can say can change
  anything now
Because there's just different people
  coming down here now
And they see things in different ways
And soon everything we've known will
  just be swept away

So say good-bye, it's Independence Day
Papa now I know the things you wanted
  that you could not say
But won't you just say good-bye, it's
  Independence Day
I swear I never meant to take those
  things away

hungry
heart

Got a wife and kids in Baltimore, Jack
I went out for a ride and I never went
   back
Like a river that don't know where it's
   flowing
I took a wrong turn and I just kept
   going

CHORUS:
Everybody's got a hungry heart
Everybody's got a hungry heart
Lay down your money and you play your
   part
Everybody's got a hungry heart

I met her in a Kingstown bar
We fell in love, I knew it had to end
We took what we had and we ripped it
   apart
Now here I am down in Kingstown again

(CHORUS)

Everybody needs a place to rest
Everybody wants to have a home
Don't make no difference what nobody
   says
Ain't nobody like to be alone

(CHORUS)

out in the street

Put on your best dress, baby
And darlin', fix your hair up right
'Cause there's a party, honey
Way down beneath the neon lights
All day you've been working that hard
    line
Now tonight you're gonna have a good
    time

I work five days a week, girl
Loading crates down on the dock
I take my hard-earned money
And meet my girl down on the block
And Monday when the foreman calls
    time
I've already got Friday on my mind

When that whistle blows
Girl, I'm down the street
I'm home, I'm out of my work clothes
When I'm out in the street
I walk the way I wanna walk

When I'm out in the street
I talk the way I wanna talk
When I'm out in the street
When I'm out in the street

When I'm out in the street, girl
Well I never feel alone
When I'm out in the street, girl
In the crowd I feel at home
The black and whites they cruise by
And they watch us from the corner of
    their eye

But there ain't no doubt, girl, down here
We ain't gonna take what they're
    handing out
When I'm out in the street
I walk the way I wanna walk
When I'm out in the street
I talk the way I wanna talk
Baby, out in the street I don't feel sad
    or blue

Baby, out in the street I'll be waiting
    for you

When that whistle blows
Girl, I'm down the street
I'm home, I'm out of my work clothes
When I'm out in the street
I walk the way I wanna walk
When I'm out in the street
I talk the way I wanna talk

When I'm out in the street
Pretty girls they're all passing by
When I'm out in the street
From the corner we give them the eye

Baby, out in the street I just feel all
    right
Meet me out in the street, little girl,
    tonight
Meet me out in the street
Meet me out in the street

crush on you

My feets were flyin' down the street just
the other night
When a Hong Kong special pulled up at
the light
What was inside, man, was just *c'est
magnifique*
I wanted to hold the bumper and let her
drag me down the street

CHORUS:
Ooh, ooh, I got a crush on you
Ooh, ooh, I got a crush on you
Ooh, ooh, I got a crush on you tonight

Sometimes I spot a little stranger
standing 'cross the room
My brain takes a vacation just to give
my heart more room
For one kiss, darling, I swear everything
I would give

'Cause you're a walking, talking reason
to live

(CHORUS)

Well now she might be the talk of high
society
She's probably got a lousy personality
She might be a heiress to Rockefeller
She might be a waitress or a bank
teller
She makes the Venus de Milo look like
she's got no style
She makes Sheena of the Jungle look
meek and mild
I need a quick shot, doc, knock me off
my feet
'Cause I'll be minding my own business
walking down the street . . .
watch out

(CHORUS)

Overleaf: Rehearsing for *The River* album, Holmdel, New Jersey

you can look [but you better not touch]

Yesterday I went shopping, buddy,
    down to the mall
Looking for something pretty I could
    hang on my wall
I knocked over a lamp, before it hit the
    floor I caught it
A salesman turned around said "Boy,
    you break that thing, you bought it"

CHORUS:
You can look but you better not touch,
    boy
You can look but you better not touch,
    boy
Mess around and you'll end up in
    Dutch, boy
You can look but you better not, no you
    better not, no you better not touch

When I came home from work and I
switched on channel five
There was a pretty little girly lookin'
    straight into my eyes
Well I watched as she wiggled back and
    forth across the screen
She didn't get me excited, she just
    made me feel mean

(CHORUS)

Well I called up Dirty Annie on the tele-
    phone
I took her out to the drive-in just to get
    her alone
I found a lovers' rendezvous, the music
    low, set to park
I heard a tappin' on the window and a
    voice in the dark

(CHORUS)

i wanna marry you

I see you walking, baby, down the street
Pushing that baby carriage at your feet
I see that lonely ribbon in your hair
Tell me am I the man for whom you put
    it there

You never smile, girl, you never speak
You just walk on by, darlin', week after
    week
Raising two kids alone in this mixed-up
    world
Must be a lonely life for a working girl

CHORUS:
Little girl I wanna marry you
Oh yeah, little girl, I wanna marry you
Yes I do, little girl, I wanna marry you

Now honey I don't want to clip your
    wings
But a time comes when two people
    should think of these things
Having a home and a family

Facing up to their responsibilities
They say in the end true love prevails
But in the end true love can't be some
    fairy tale
To say I'll make your dreams come true
    would be wrong
But maybe, darlin', I could help them
    along

(CHORUS)

My daddy said right before he died
That true, true love was just a lie
He went to his grave a broken heart
An unfulfilled life, girl, makes a man
    hard

Oh darlin'
There's something happy and there's
    something sad
'Bout wanting somebody oh so bad
I wear my love, darlin', without shame
I'd be proud if you would wear my name

the river

I come from down in the valley
Where mister, when you're young
They bring you up to do like your daddy
    done
Me and Mary we met in high school
When she was just seventeen
We'd drive out of this valley
Down to where the fields were green
We'd go down to the river
And into the river we'd dive
Oh down to the river we'd ride

Then I got Mary pregnant
And man, that was all she wrote
And for my nineteenth birthday
I got a union card and a wedding coat
We went down to the courthouse
And the judge put it all to rest
No wedding day smiles, no walk down
    the aisle
No flowers, no wedding dress
That night we went down to the river
And into the river we'd dive
Oh down to the river we did ride

I got a job working construction
For the Johnstown Company

But lately there ain't been much work
On account of the economy
Now all them things that seemed so
    important
Well mister, they vanished right into the
    air
Now I just act like I don't remember
Mary acts like she don't care
But I remember us riding in my
    brother's car
Her body tan and wet down at the
    reservoir
At night on them banks I'd lie awake
And pull her close just to feel each
    breath she'd take
Now those memories come back to
    haunt me
They haunt me like a curse
Is a dream a lie if it don't come true
Or is it something worse
That sends me down to the river
Though I know the river is dry
That sends me down to the river tonight
Down to the river
My baby and I
Oh down to the river we ride

point blank

Do you still say your prayers, little
  darlin'
Do you go to bed at night
Prayin' that tomorrow everything will be
  all right
But tomorrows fall in number
In number one by one
You wake up and you're dying
You don't even know what from
Well they shot you point blank
You been shot in the back
Baby, point blank
You been fooled this time, little girl,
  that's a fact
Right between the eyes, baby, point
  blank
Right between the pretty lies that
  they tell
Little girl you fell

You grew up where young girls they
  grow up fast
You took what you were handed and left
  behind what was asked
But what they asked, baby, wasn't right
You didn't have to live that life
I was gonna be your Romeo, you were
  gonna be my Juliet
These days you don't wait on Romeos,
  you wait on that welfare check
And on all the pretty little things that
  you can't ever have

And on all the promises
That always end up point blank
Shot between the eyes
Point blank
Like little white lies you tell to ease the
  pain
You're walkin' in the sights, girl, of
  point blank
And it's one false move and baby the
  lights go out

Once I dreamed we were together again
Baby, you and me
Back home in those old clubs
The way we used to be
We were standin' at the bar and it was
  hard to hear
The band was playin' loud and you
  were shoutin' something in my ear
You pulled my jacket off and as the
  drummer counted four
You grabbed my hand and pulled me
  out on the floor
You just stood there and held me, then
  you started dancin' slow
And as I pulled you tighter I swore I'd
  never let you go
Well I saw you last night down on the
  avenue
Your face was in the shadows but I
  knew that it was you

You were standin' in the doorway out of
  the rain
You didn't answer when I called out
  your name
You just turned and then you looked
  away
Like just another stranger waitin' to get
  blown away
Point blank
Right between the eyes
Point blank
Right between the pretty lies you fell
Point blank
Shot straight through the heart
Yeah, point blank
You've been twisted up till you've
  become just another part of it
Point blank
You're walkin' in the sights
Point blank
Livin' one false move just one false
  move away
Point blank
They caught you in their sights
Point blank
Did you forget how to love, girl, did you
  forget how to fight
Point blank
They must have shot you in the head
'Cause point blank
Bang bang baby you're dead

cadillac ranch

Well there she sits, buddy, just
    a-gleamin' in the sun
There to greet a working man when his
    day is done
I'm gonna pack my pa and I'm gonna
    pack my aunt
I'm gonna take them down to the
    Cadillac Ranch

Eldorado fins, whitewalls and skirts
Rides just like a little bit of heaven
    here on earth
Well buddy when I die throw my body in
    the back
And drive me to the junkyard in my
    Cadillac

Cadillac, Cadillac
Long and dark, shiney and black
Open up your engines, let 'em roar
Tearing up the highway like a big old
    dinosaur

James Dean in that Mercury '49
Junior Johnson runnin' through the
    woods of Caroline

Even Burt Reynolds in that black
    TransAm
All gonna meet down at the Cadillac
    Ranch

Cadillac, Cadillac
Long and dark, shiney and black
Open up your engines, let 'em roar
Tearing up the highway like a big old
    dinosaur

Hey little girlie in the blue jeans so
    tight
Drivin' alone through the Wisconsin
    night
You're my last love, baby, you're my last
    chance
Don't let 'em take me to the Cadillac
    Ranch

Cadillac, Cadillac
Long and dark, shiney and black
Pulled up to my house today
Came and took my little girl away

i'm a rocker

I got a .007 watch and it's a one and
only
It's got a *I Spy* beeper that tells me
when you're lonely
I got a Batmobile so I can reach you in
a fast shake
When your world's in crisis of an
impendin' heartbreak

Now don't you call James Bond or
Secret Agent Man
'Cause they can't do it like I can
I'm a rocker, baby, I'm a rocker—every
day
I'm a rocker, baby, I'm a rocker

If you're hanging from a cliff or you're
tied to the tracks, girl
Columbo split and you can't find Kojak
True love is broken and your tears are
fallin' faster
You're sufferin' from a pain in your
heart or some other natural disaster

Now I don't care what kind of shape
you're in
If they put up a roadblock I'll parachute
in

I'm a rocker, baby, I'm a rocker—I'm in
love
I'm a rocker, baby, I'm a rocker—every
day
I'm a rocker, baby, I'm a rocker—with
you

So you fell for some jerk who was tall,
dark and handsome
Then he kidnapped your heart and now
he's holdin' it for ransom
Well like a *Mission Impossible* I'm
gonna go and get it back
You know I woulda taken better care of
it, baby, than that

Sometimes I get so hot, girl, well I
can't talk
But when I'm with you I cool off
I'm a rocker, baby, I'm a rocker—and I
walk
I'm a rocker, baby, I'm a rocker—and I
talk
I'm a rocker, baby, I'm a rocker—every
day
I'm a rocker, baby, I'm a rocker—every
day

fade away

Well now you say you've found another
   man
Who does things to you that I can't
And that no matter what I do it's all
   over now
Between me and you, girl
But I can't believe what you say
No I can't believe what you say
'Cause baby

CHORUS:
I don't wanna fade away
Oh I don't wanna fade away
Tell me what can I do, what can I say
'Cause darlin' I don't wanna fade away

Well now you say that you've made up
   your mind it's been such a long, long
   time since it's been good with us
And that somewhere back along the
   line you lost your love and I lost your
   trust
Now rooms that once were so bright
Are filled with the coming night, darlin'

(CHORUS)

You say it's not easy for you
And that you've been so lonely
While other girls go out doing what they
   want to do
You say that you miss the nights
When we'd go out dancing
The days when you and I walked as two
Well girl I miss them too
Oh I swear that I do
Oh girl

Now baby I don't wanna be just another
   useless memory holding you tight
Or just some other ghost out on the
   street to whom you stop and politely
   speak when you pass on by
Vanishing into the night
Left to vanish into the night
No baby

(CHORUS)

stolen
car

I met a little girl and I settled down
In a little house out on the edge of
    town
We got married and swore we'd never
    part
Then little by little we drifted from each
    other's heart

At first I thought it was just restless-
    ness
That would fade as time went by and
    our love grew deep
In the end it was something more I
    guess
That tore us apart and made us weep

And I'm driving a stolen car
Down on Eldridge Avenue
Each night I wait to get caught
But I never do

She asked if I remembered the letters I
    wrote
When our love was young and bold
She said last night she read those
    letters
And they made her feel one hundred
    years old

And I'm driving a stolen car
On a pitch-black night
And I'm telling myself I'm gonna be all
    right
But I ride by night and I travel in fear
That in this darkness I will disappear

ramrod

Hey little dolly with the blue jeans on
I wanna ramrod with you, honey, till
    half-past dawn
Let your hair down, mama, and pick up
    this beat
Come on and meet me tonight down on
    Bluebird Street
I've been working all week, I'm up to my
    neck in hock
Come Saturday night I let my ramrod
    rock

She's a hot-stepping hemi with a four
    on the floor
She's a roadrunner engine in a '32 Ford
Late at night when I'm dead on the line
I swear I think of your pretty face when
    I let her unwind
Well look over yonder, see them city
    lights

Come on little dolly 'n' go ramroddin'
    tonight

Come on, come on, come on little baby
Come on, come on, let's shake it tonight
Come on, come on, come on little sugar
Dance with your daddy and we'll go
    ramroddin' tonight

Hey little dolly won't you say you will
Meet me tonight up on top of the hill
Well just a few miles 'cross the county
    line
There's a cute little chapel nestled
    down in the pines
Say you'll be mine, little girl, I'll put my
    foot to the floor
Give me the word now, sugar, we'll go
    ramroddin' forevermore

the price you pay

You make up your mind, you choose the
chance you take
You ride to where the highway ends and
the desert breaks
Out on to an open road you ride until
the day
You learn to sleep at night with the
price you pay

Now with their hands held high they
reached out for the open skies
And in one last breath they built the
roads they'd ride to their death
Driving on through the night, unable to
break away
From the restless pull of the price you
pay

CHORUS:

Oh the price you pay, oh the price you
pay
Now you can't walk away from the price
you pay

Now they'd come so far and they'd
waited so long
Just to end up caught in a dream where
everything goes wrong
Where the dark of night holds back the
light of the day
And you've gotta stand and fight for the
price you pay

(CHORUS)

Little girl down on the strand
With that pretty little baby in your
hands

Do you remember the story of the
promised land
How he crossed the desert sands
And could not enter the chosen land
On the banks of the river he stayed
To face the price you pay

So let the game start, you better run,
you little wild heart
You can run through all the nights and
all the days
But just across the county line
A stranger passing through put up a
sign
That counts the men fallen away
To the price you pay
And girl before the end of the day
I'm gonna tear it down and throw it
away

drive all night

When I lost you, honey, sometimes I
   think I lost my guts too
And I wish God would send me a word,
   send me something I'm afraid to
   lose
Lying in the heat of the night like
   prisoners all our lives
I get shivers down my spine
And all I wanna do is hold you tight

CHORUS:
I swear I'd drive all night again
Just to buy you some shoes
And to taste your tender charms
And I just wanna sleep tonight again in
   your arms

Tonight there's fallen angels and
   they're waiting for us down in the
   street
Tonight there's calling strangers, hear
   them crying in defeat

Let them go, let them go, let them go
   do their dances of the dead (let 'em
   go right ahead)
You just dry your eyes and c'mon,
   c'mon, c'mon, let's go to bed, baby,
   baby, baby

(CHORUS)

There's machines and there's fire, baby,
   waiting on the edge of town
They're out there for hire but baby, they
   can't hurt us now
'Cause you've got, you've got, you've
   got my love, you've got my love, girl
Through the wind, through the rain, the
   snow, the wind, the rain
You've got, you've got my love
Heart and soul

wreck on the highway

Last night I was out driving
Coming home at the end of the working
   day
I was riding alone through the drizzling
   rain
On a deserted stretch of a county two-
   lane
When I came upon a wreck on the
   highway

There was blood and glass all over
And there was nobody there but me
As the rain tumbled down hard and
   cold
I seen a young man lying by the side of
   the road
He cried "Mister, won't you help me
   please?"

An ambulance finally came and took
   him to Riverside
I watched as they drove him away
And I thought of a girlfriend or a young
   wife
And a state trooper knocking in the
   middle of the night
To say your baby died in a wreck on the
   highway

Sometimes I sit up in the darkness
And I watch my baby as she sleeps
Then I climb in bed and I hold her tight
I just lay there awake in the middle of
   the night
Thinking 'bout the wreck on the
   highway

nebraska

By 1981, after a year of touring around the world for *The River,* I came back to New Jersey and began thinking about my next record. I'd grown tired of expending so much energy in professional recording studios where I rarely got the right group of songs I was after without wasting a lot of time and expense. I found the atmosphere in the studio to be sterile and isolating, and the long drifting records emotionally wearing. I decided I needed to find a way to hear my songs before I brought them into the studio.

I called my guitar tech and asked him to pick up something that would be suitable for some cheap and easy home recording. He came back with a four-track Teac tape machine, and we set it up in my bedroom in Colts Neck, New Jersey. That was where I recorded *Nebraska.*

The songs on *Nebraska* connected to my childhood more than any other record I'd made. The tone of the music was directly linked to what I remembered of my early youth. We lived with my grandparents until I was six. Thinking through these songs, I went back and recalled what that time felt like, particularly my grandmother's house. There was something about the walls, the lack of decoration, the almost painful plainness.

Our house was heated by a single kerosene stove in the living room. One of my earliest childhood memories was the smell of kerosene and my grandfather standing there filling the spout in the rear of the stove. All of our cooking was done on a coal stove in the kitchen. As a child, I'd shoot my watergun at its hot, iron surface and watch the steam rise.

The centerpiece of our living room was a single photo of my father's older sister who died at the age of five in a bicycle accident around the corner by the local gas station. Her ethereal presence from this 1920s portrait gave the room a feeling of being lost in time.

At home, just before recording *Nebraska*, I was reading Flannery O'Connor. Her stories reminded me of the unknowability of God and contained a dark spirituality that resonated with my own feelings at the time. Film continued to be an influence. I'd recently seen *True Confessions* and Terrence Malick's *Badlands*. There was a stillness on the surface of those pictures, while underneath lay a world of moral ambiguity and violence.

The songs were written relatively quickly because they all rose from the same ground. They took three, maybe four takes to record. Some, like "Highway Patrolman" and "State Trooper," only one. But most everything was done in no more than a few weeks. "Mansion on the Hill," which I had the beginning of for some time, was the first song I finished; "My Father's House" was the last.

there is all sorts of stuff here. what I
did is put anything on I thought would be good for you
to hear. I still left off about 5 or 7 things that
I had I finished or really wanted the band to work
out with. Many of the songs may need editing, lines
changed, arrangement changes. Some will really work, others
may just need to be put aside but there was something in
each one I got a kick out of so it's included. I got
a lot of ideas but I'm not exactly sure of where I'm
going. I guess the only thing I looked for in the songs
was that it someway break a little new ground for
me. they all don't do this some I just got a blast out of
but I think a good amount do or at least try.

they may not hit you right away, or they may sound
a little foreign. they were mostly all written from the
time we got off tour to right before christmas, about
3½ months. So here it is!

From the cover letter sent to Jon Landau with the *Nebraska* tape.

When I wrote "Nebraska," my retelling of the Charles Starkweather–Caril Fugate 1950s murder spree, I'd found the record's center. The songs tapped into white gospel and early Appalachian music, as well as the blues. In small detail—the slow twirling of a baton, the twisting of a ring on a finger—they found their character. I often wrote from a child's point of view: "Mansion on the Hill," "Used Cars," "My Father's House"— these were all stories that came directly out of my experience with my family.

The songs had religious and political over-tones, but more importantly, I was trying to get them to sound right. That's what would deepen the images. I thought of John Lee Hooker and Robert Johnson—records that sounded so good with the lights out. I wanted to let the listener hear the characters think, to get inside their heads, so you could hear and feel their thoughts, their choices.

1. Bye Bye Johnny
2. Starkweather (Nebraska)
3. Atlanta City
4. Mansion on the Hill
5. Born in the USA.
6. Johnny 99
7. Downbound Train
8. Losin Kind
9. State Trooper
10. Used Cars
11. Wanda (open All Night)
12. Child Bride
13. Pink Cadillac
14. Highway Patrolman
15. Reason to Believe

Early song lineup for *Nebraska*

There was a natural link between the songs on *The River* and those on *Nebraska.* "Stolen Car," "Wreck on the Highway," "Point Blank," and "The River" reflected a shift in my songwriting style. My *Nebraska* songs were the opposite of the rock music I'd been writing. These new songs were narrative, restrained, linear, and musically minimal. Yet their depiction of characters out on the edge contextualized them as rock and roll.

If there's a theme that runs through the record, it's the thin line between stability and that moment when time stops and everything goes to black, when the things that connect you to your

world—your job, your family, friends, your faith, the love and grace in your heart—fail you. I

wanted the music to feel like a waking dream and the record to move like poetry. I wanted the

blood on it to feel destined and fateful.

All popular artists get caught between making records and making music. If you're lucky, some-

times it's the same thing. When you learn to craft your music into recordings, there's always

something gained and lost. The ease of an unselfconscious voice gives way to the formality of

presentation. On certain records, that may enhance the music you're making and help you find

a receptive audience. On other records, it may destroy the essential nature of what you've done.

I sat in a chair, singing and playing into a couple of microphones. With the two tracks left,

after I sang and played the song, I could add a harmony or hit the tambourine. Sometimes I

added a guitar. On four tracks that was all you could do. I mixed it through a guitar echoplex

unit onto a beat box, like the one you take to the beach. They were just "demos." After that, I

went into the studio, brought in the band, rerecorded, remixed, and succeeded in making the

whole thing worse. Finally satisfied that I'd explored all the music's possibilities, I pulled the

original home-recorded cassette out of my jeans pocket where I'd been carrying it and said, "This

is it."

1. Bye Bye Johnny - no explanation necessary.
2. Starkweather or Nebraska - 4 mixes
   ① with 12 string - complete version this song may need
editing or verses switched but it might be right as it is.
this is about the Charles Starkweather murder spree in Nebraska in
the 50's.   mix ② early fade ③ bad harp no good 4. with glock
3. Atlantic City - 3 different takes - all with slight lyric changes *+ arrange.
   ① #1 take ② #3 ③ #4 this song should probably be done with
whole band + really rockin out.

skip → 4. this song comes #6 on the tape
   ~~Mansion on the Hill~~ - Johnny 99 - 2 versions, kinda fun!
these words are not completely worked out or finished + so
the singing is occasionally awkward. I don't know if this
song is a keeper or not but I thought you'd get a kick
out of it. ① #2 ② #3 different end verse

4.) Mansion on the Hill -

                                                      3 mixes
         and with slight balance change / 1st 2 mixes are a
         little dirty 3rd is best recording quality
5. Born in the U.S.A. - you sent me the paul schrader script
         which I did not have a chance to read yet but I did
         whip up this little ditty purloining it's title. On this number

         song should be done very hard rockin. this song is in very
         rough shape but is as good as I can get it at the moment it might have potential -
6. Johnny 99 - see above

7. Down Bound Train - uptempo rocker for full effect
              needs band / could be exciting
8. Losin Kind - searched + searched for a better side,
         spent many hours on this task but no good.

Song summary sent to Jon Landau with the *Nebraska* tape

I like the verses but I can't seem to find a better punch line
kind of like a James M. Cain story
could be done with more of a band arrangement
3 Takes - all slight lyric changes (last verse)

9. State Trooper - I dreamed this one up comin back
from New York one night I don't know if it's even
really a song or not but I did it so I figured I'd
throw it on. It's kinda weird

10. Used Cars - the exciting story of my own personal life
2 Takes 1st is a little dirt recording wise and cleaner

11. Wanda (Open All Night) in which the hero braves
snow sleet rain + the highway patrol for a kiss from
his baby's lips. this song is very hard to perform and more voice 2 Takes

12. the Child Bride - in which the protagonist violates
the Mann Act ~~xxxxxxx~~ and is left to
ponder his fate. this is kind of a work in progress or
more like without progress. I worked a real long time on
this song and could never quite get it right. I spent so much
time on it I thought I'd include it a see what you think

13. Pink Cadillac - self explanatory

14. Highway Patrolman - this is the same as "Child Bride"
and to a lesser degree "losin kind. worked very long on
this and always had the feeling I was comin up short.
not really finished but is about as good as I can get it at the
time. Don't think the ending was quite strong enough

15. Reason To Believe - No not the Tim Hardin song
but a completely original tune by the same name
culled from my own experience driving down Highway 33
on my way to Millstone. 2 Takes second has
extra verse

nebraska

I saw her standin' on her front lawn
   just twirlin' her baton
Me and her went for a ride, sir, and ten
   innocent people died

From the town of Lincoln, Nebraska,
   with a sawed-off .410 on my lap
Through the badlands of Wyoming I
   killed everything in my path

I can't say that I'm sorry for the things
   that we done
At least for a little while, sir, me and
   her we had us some fun

The jury brought in a guilty verdict and
   the judge he sentenced me to death
Midnight in a prison storeroom with
   leather straps across my chest

Sheriff, when the man pulls that
   switch, sir, and snaps my poor head
   back
You make sure my pretty baby is sittin'
   right there on my lap

They declared me unfit to live, said into
   that great void my soul'd be hurled
They wanted to know why I did what I
   did, well, sir, guess there's just a
   meanness in this world

atlantic city

Well they blew up the chicken man in
  Philly last night
Now they blew up his house too
Down on the boardwalk they're gettin'
  ready for a fight
Gonna see what them racket boys
  can do

Now there's trouble busin' in from outta
  state
And the D.A. can't get no relief
Gonna be a rumble out on the
  promenade
And the gamblin' commissioner's
  hangin' on by the skin of his teeth

CHORUS:
Everything dies, baby, that's a fact

But maybe everything that dies some
  day comes back
Put your makeup on, fix your hair up
  pretty
And meet me tonight in Atlantic City

Well I got a job and tried to put my
  money away
But I got debts that no honest man
  can pay
So I drew what I had from the Central
  Trust
And I bought us two tickets on that
  Coast City bus

(CHORUS)

Now our luck may have died and our
  love may be cold

But with you forever I'll stay
We're goin' out where the sand's turnin'
  to gold
So put on your stockings 'cause the
  night's gettin' cold

(CHORUS)

Now I been lookin' for a job but it's hard
  to find
Down here it's just winners and losers
  and don't get caught on the wrong
  side of that line
Well I'm tired of comin' out on the losin'
  end
So honey last night I met this guy and
  I'm gonna do a little favor for him

(CHORUS)

Atlantic City

They blew up the chicken man in Philly last night

they blew up his house too

down on the boardwalk they're getting ready for a fight

gonna see what them racket boys do

(2) 1 now I got a job and I tried to put my money away

    2 judge I got debts no honest man can pay

    3 so I ~~bought~~ drew all my money from the Central Trust

    4 I bought 2 tickets on that Greyhound bus

(2)(3) 5. Now my luck may have died and my love may be cold

    we can get it all back I feel it I know it

    but baby I swear I'll see the day

[(2) 1 so put your stockings on honey cause the night's getting cold

2 or 4 & we're going out where the sands turning to gold

Now I got a job and I tried to put my money away

but judge I had debts no honest man can pay

3 or 1 ya get tired of comin out on the losin end

4 or 2 honey last night I met this guy and I'm gonna do a little

    favor for him   I guess everything dies

(4)(3) 6. the end of his story I ain't told

down here it's just winners & losers & don't get caught on the wrong

    side of that line

there's money to be made do be what I do be afraid

down here poor ... in 2 kinds

mansion on the hill

There's a place out on the edge of town,
    sir
Risin' above the factories and the fields
Now ever since I was a child I can
    remember
That mansion on the hill

In the day you can see the children
    playing
On the road that leads to those gates of
    hardened steel
Steel gates that completely surround,
    sir
The mansion on the hill

At night my daddy'd take me and we'd
    ride
Through the streets of a town so silent
    and still

Park on a back road along the high-
    way side
Look up at that mansion on the hill

In the summer all the lights would
    shine
There'd be music playin', people
    laughin' all the time
Me and my sister we'd hide out in the
    tall corn fields
Sit and listen to the mansion on the
    hill

Tonight down here in Linden town
I watch the cars rushin' by home from
    the mill
There's a beautiful full moon rising
Above the mansion on the hill

1. they'd closed down the auto plant in Mahwah late that month
~~John~~ Ralph went out lookin for a job but he couldn't find none
he came home too drunk from mixin Tanqueray + wine
got a gun shot a night clerk now they call him Johnny 99

down in the part of town where if you don't stop
he was wavin a gun around screamin he was gonna blow his top
an off duty cop snuck up on Johnny from behind
in front of the club Tiny Tip they slapped the cuffs on Johnny 99

the court supplied a public defender but the judge was mean old John Brown
he walked into the courtroom + stared poor Johnny down
the evidence is clear gonna let the sentence son fit the crime
death in the chair and well call it even Johnny 99

A brawl broke ~~out~~ court room feels flew by dry Johny dad away   wifey Gurl
the court room ~~broke out~~ was in an uproar they had to drag Johny's folks away
his momma stood up + screamed ~~shouted~~ judge don't take my ~~good~~ boy he was/ ~~cried~~
I'm sorry mam but the law must be satisfied
(at the (murder) ~~killin~~ hands if yur son an honest man ~~man~~ died)
son is there a statement you'd like to make before you die

                    got a wife + kids + responsibilities
judge I worked the assembly line since I was 18
the bank told my mortgage + they was comin down hard on me
now I ain't sayin that ~~I'm~~ makes me an innocent man
but it was more than all this that put that gun in my hand

johnny 99

Well they closed down the auto plant in
    Mahwah late that month
Ralph went out lookin' for a job but he
    couldn't find none
He came home too drunk from mixin'
    Tanqueray and wine
He got a gun, shot a night clerk, now
    they call 'im Johnny 99

Down in the part of town where when
    you hit a red light you don't stop
Johnny's wavin' his gun around and
    threatenin' to blow his top
When an off-duty cop snuck up on him
    from behind
Out in front of the Club Tip Top they
    slapped the cuffs on Johnny 99

Well the city supplied a public defender
    but the judge was Mean John Brown
He came into the courtroom and stared
    poor Johnny down
Well the evidence is clear, gonna let the
    sentence, son, fit the crime
Prison for ninety-eight and a year and
    we'll call it even Johnny 99

A fistfight broke out in the courtroom,
    they had to drag Johnny's girl away
His mama stood up and shouted "Judge
    don't take my boy this way"
Well son, you got a statement you'd like
    to make
Before the bailiff comes to forever take
    you away

Now judge, I got debts no honest man
    could pay
The bank was holdin' my mortgage and
    they was takin' my house away
Now I ain't sayin' that makes me an
    innocent man
But it was more 'n' all this that put
    that gun in my hand
Well your honor, I do believe I'd be
    better off dead
And if you can take a man's life for the
    thoughts that's in his head
Then won't you sit back in that chair
    and think it over, judge, one more
    time
And let 'em shave off my hair and put
    me on that execution line

highway patrolman

My name is Joe Roberts, I work for the
state
I'm a sergeant out of Perrineville,
barracks number eight
I always done an honest job, as honest
as I could
I got a brother named Frankie and
Frankie ain't no good

Now ever since we was young kids it's
been the same comedown
I get a call over the shortwave Frankie's
in trouble downtown
Well if it was any other man I'd just put
him straight away
But when it's your brother sometimes
you look the other way

Me and Frankie laughin' and drinkin'
Nothin' feels better than blood on blood
Takin' turns dancin' with Maria
As the band played "Night of the
Johnstown Flood"
I catch him when he's strayin' like any
brother would
Man turns his back on his family, well
he just ain't no good

Well Frankie went in the army back in
1965
I got a farm deferment, settled down,
took Maria for my wife
But them wheat prices kept on droppin'
Till it was like we were gettin' robbed
Frankie came home in '68 and me I
took this job

Yeah, we're laughin' and drinkin'
Nothin' feels better than blood on blood
Takin' turns dancin' with Maria
As the band played "Night of the
Johnstown Flood"
I catch him when he's strayin', teach
him how to walk that line
Man turns his back on his family, he
ain't no friend of mine

The night was like any other, I got a call
'bout quarter to nine
There was trouble in a roadhouse out on
the Michigan line
There was a kid lyin' on the floor lookin'
bad, bleedin' hard from his head
There was a girl cryin' at a table, it was
Frank, they said

Well I went out and I jumped in my car
and I hit the lights
I must of drove 110 through Michigan
county that night
It was out at the crossroads down
'round Willow bank
Seen a Buick with Ohio plates, behind
the wheel was Frank
Well I chased him through them county
roads till a sign said "Canadian
border 5 miles from here"
I pulled over the side of the highway
and watched his taillights disappear

Me and Frankie laughin' and drinkin'
Nothin' feels better than blood on blood
Takin' turns dancin' with Maria
As the band played "Night of the
Johnstown Flood"
I catch him when he's strayin' like any
brother would
Man turns his back on his family, well
he just ain't no good

state
trooper

New Jersey Turnpike, ridin' on a wet
  night
'Neath the refinery's glow out where the
  great black rivers flow
License, registration, I ain't got none
But I got a clear conscience 'bout the
  things that I done
Mister state trooper, please don't stop
  me

Maybe you got a kid, maybe you got a
  pretty wife
The only thing that I got's been
  botherin' me my whole life
Mister state trooper, please don't stop
  me

In the wee wee hours your mind gets
  hazy
Radio relay towers lead me to my baby
Radio's jammed up with talk show
  stations
It's just talk talk talk talk till you lose
  your patience
Mister state trooper, please don't stop
  me

Hey somebody out there, listen to my
  last prayer
Hi ho silver-o deliver me from nowhere

used cars

My little sister's in the front seat with
   an ice cream cone
My ma's in the backseat sittin' all alone
As my pa steers her slow out of the lot
For a test drive down Michigan Avenue

Now my ma she fingers her wedding
   band
And watches the salesman stare at my
   old man's hands
He's tellin' us all 'bout the break he'd
   give us if he could but he just can't
Well if I could I swear I know just what
   I'd do

Now mister, the day the lottery I win
I ain't ever gonna ride in no used car
   again

Now the neighbors come from near and
   far

As we pull up in our brand-new used
   car
I wish he'd just hit the gas and let out
   a cry
And tell 'em all they can kiss our asses
   good-bye

My dad he sweats the same job from
   mornin' to morn
Me I walk home on the same dirty
   streets where I was born
Up the block I can hear my little sister
   in the front seat blowin' that horn
The sounds echo all down Michigan
   Avenue

Now mister, the day my number comes
   in
I ain't ever gonna ride in no used car
   again

open all night

I had the carburetor cleaned and
  checked
With her line blown out she's hummin'
  like a turbojet
Propped her up in the backyard on
  concrete blocks
For a new clutch plate and a new set of
  shocks
Took her down to the carwash, check
  the plugs and points
I'm goin' out tonight, I'm gonna rock
  that joint

Early north Jersey industrial skyline
I'm a all-set Cobra jet creepin' through
  the nighttime
Gotta find a gas station, gotta find a
  pay phone
This turnpike sure is spooky at night
  when you're all alone
Gotta hit the gas 'cause I'm runnin'
  late
This New Jersey in the mornin' like a
  lunar landscape

The boss don't dig me so he put me on
  the night shift
It's an all-night run to get back to
  where my baby lives
In the wee wee hours your mind gets
  hazy
Radio relay towers, won't you lead me
  to my baby
Underneath the overpass trooper hits
  his party light switch
Goodnight, good luck, one two power-
  shift

I met Wanda when she was employed
Behind the counter at the Route 60
  Bob's Big Boy
Fried chicken on the front seat, she's
  sittin' in my lap
We're wipin' our fingers on a Texaco
  road map
I remember Wanda up on Scrap Metal
  Hill
With them big brown eyes that make
  your heart stand still

Five A.M., oil pressure's sinkin' fast
I make a pit stop, wipe the windshield,
  check the gas
Gotta call my baby on the telephone
Let her know that her daddy's comin' on
  home
Sit tight, little mama, I'm comin' 'round
I got three more hours but I'm coverin'
  ground

Your eyes get itchy in the wee wee
  hours
Sun's just a red ball risin' over them
  refinery towers
Radio's jammed up with gospel stations
Lost souls callin' long distance
  salvation
Hey Mr. Deejay, won'tcha hear my last
  prayer
Hey ho, rock and roll, deliver me from
  nowhere

my father's house

Last night I dreamed that I was a child
Out where the pines grow wild and tall
I was trying to make it home through
    the forest
Before the darkness falls

I heard the wind rustling through the
    trees
And ghostly voices rose from the fields
I ran with my heart pounding down that
    broken path
With the devil snappin' at my heels

I broke through the trees and there in
    the night
My father's house stood shining hard
    and bright
The branches and brambles tore my
    clothes and scratched my arms
But I ran till I fell shaking in his arms

I awoke and I imagined the hard things
    that pulled us apart

Will never again, sir, tear us from each
    other's hearts
I got dressed and to that house I did
    ride
From out on the road I could see its
    window shining in light

I walked up the steps and stood on the
    porch
A woman I didn't recognize came and
    spoke to me through a chained door
I told her my story and who I'd come for
She said "I'm sorry, son, but no one by
    that name lives here anymore"

My father's house shines hard and
    bright
It stands like a beacon calling me in
    the night
Calling and calling so cold and alone
Shining 'cross this dark highway where
    our sins lie unatoned

reason to believe

Seen a man standin' over a dead dog
   lyin' by the highway in a ditch
He's lookin' down kinda puzzled pokin'
   that dog with a stick
Got his car door flung open, he's
   standin' out on Highway 31
Like if he stood there long enough that
   dog'd get up and run
Struck me kinda funny, seem kinda
   funny, sir, to me
Still at the end of every hard day people
   find some reason to believe

Now Mary Lou loved Johnny with a love
   mean and true
She said "Baby I'll work for you every
   day and bring my money home
   to you"

One day he up and left her and ever
   since that
She waits down at the end of that dirt
   road for young Johnny to come back
Struck me kinda funny, funny, yeah,
   indeed
How at the end of every hard-earned
   day people find some reason to
   believe

Take a baby to the river, Kyle William
   they called him
Wash the baby in the water, take away
   little Kyle's sin
In a whitewash shotgun shack an old
   man passes away
Take the body to the graveyard and over
   him they pray

Lord won't you tell us, tell us what does
   it mean
At the end of every hard-earned day you
   can find some reason to believe

Congregation gathers down by the river
   side
Preacher stands with a Bible, groom
   stands waitin' for his bride
Congregation gone and the sun sets
   behind a weepin' willow tree
Groom stands alone and watches the
   river rush on so effortlessly
Wonderin' where can his baby be
Still at the end of every hard-earned day
   people find some reason to believe

born
in
the
u.s.a.

n 1981 director Paul Schrader sent me a script called *Born in the U.S.A.*—a film revolving around the lives of some fictional local musicians in Cleveland. He wanted me to come up with some music for the film. But the script sat on my writing table until one day I was singing a new song I was writing called "Vietnam." I looked over and sang off the top of Paul's cover page, "I was born in the U.S.A." I had cut the song for *Nebraska* but didn't use it. Six months later I cut it with the band and that version became the title song for my next record. (I later gave Paul a song called "Light of Day," and the film was released under that title.)

The sound of "Born in the U.S.A." was martial, modal, and straight ahead. The lyrics dealt with the problems Vietnam vets faced when they came back home after fighting in "the only war that America had ever lost." In order to understand the song's intent, you needed to invest a certain amount of time and effort to absorb both the music and the words. But that's not the way a lot of

163

people use pop music. For most, music is primarily an emotional language; whatever you've written lyrically almost always comes in second to what the listener is feeling. Should form follow lyrical content? I had two experiences that illustrate how this works in the real world.

The first guy I played the finished version of "Born in the U.S.A." for was Bobby Muller, a veteran and then president of the Vietnam Veterans of America. He came into the studio and sat between two large speakers at the front of the console. I turned up the volume. He sat there for a moment listening to the first couple of verses, and then a big smile crossed his face.

Also, for years after the release of the album, at Halloween, I had little kids in red bandanas knocking at my door with their trick-or-treat bags singing, "I was born in the U.S.A." They were not particularly well-versed in the "Had a brother at Khe Sahn . . ." lyric. But they all had plenty of lung power when the chorus rolled around. I guess the same fate awaited Woody Guthrie's "This Land Is Your Land" around the campfire. But that didn't make me feel any better.

A songwriter writes to be understood. Is the way you choose to present your music its politics? Is the sound and form your song takes its content? Coming off *Nebraska,* I'd just done it both ways. On one hand, I learned a lesson about how pop and pop image is perceived. On the other hand, I wouldn't have made either of those records differently. Over the years I've had an opportunity to reinterpret "Born in the U.S.A." many times in concert. Particularly on the *Tom Joad* tour, I had a version that could not be misconstrued. But those interpretations always stood in relief to the original and gained some of their new power from the audience's previous experience with the original version. On the album, "Born in the U.S.A." was in its most powerful presenta-

tion. If I tried to undercut or change the music, I believe I would have had a record that might

have been more easily understood, but not as good.

Unlike "Born to Run," which set the mark and feel for the other songs that would make up

the album by the same name, "Born in the U.S.A." more or less stood by itself. The rest of the

album contains a group of songs about which I've always had some ambivalence.

This record was to follow *Nebraska,* which contained what I thought to have been a collec-

tion of some of my strongest songs. I wanted to take that record and electrify it. The framework

of that idea can be found on *Born in the U.S.A.* with the title song and "My Hometown." But it real-

ly didn't flesh out like I had hoped it would.

Many of the songs on the album evolved out of earlier ideas I'd had for *Nebraska.* "Born in the

U.S.A." and some part of "Downbound Train" came out of *Nebraska.* The original title for "Working on the Highway" was "Child Bride," also a song I'd written for *Nebraska.*

The rest of the songs I wrote trying to finish the album. "I'm on Fire" came to me one night in the studio when I was just goofing around with a Johnny Cash and the Tennessee Three rhythm. "My Hometown" was based on childhood memories of driving down Main Street on my dad's lap, the closing of a local mill, and a racial incident that occurred near my house in Freehold during my adolescence.

"No Surrender" was a song I didn't intend to include on the album. But Steve Van Zandt convinced me otherwise. It was a song I was uncomfortable with. You don't hold out and triumph all the time in life. You compromise, you suffer defeat; you slip into life's gray areas. But Steve talked me into putting the song on the album in the eleventh hour. He argued that the portrait of friendship and the song's expression of the inspirational power of rock music was an important part of the picture. I don't know if he was right or not, but it went on.

After Jon Landau suggested we didn't have a single for the album, I wrote "Dancing in the Dark." It went as far in the direction of pop music as I wanted to go—and probably a little farther. "Bobby Jean" was a good song about youthful friendship, and "Glory Days" was right on the money. "Darlington County," originally written for *Darkness,* was a slice-of-life road song. "Cover Me" I'd originally written for Donna Summer. She could really sing and I disliked the veiled racism of the anti-disco movement. When I cut the demo, it came out so good that I held on to it. I later wrote another song, "Protection," and recorded it with Donna and Quincy Jones in LA.

Many of these songs found themselves in concert with my audience. My heroes, from Hank Williams to Frank Sinatra to Bob Dylan, were popular musicians. They had hits. There was value in trying to connect with a large audience. It was a direct way you affected culture. It let you know how powerful and durable your music might be. But it was also risky and forced you to confront your music's limitations as well as your own.

I put a lot of pressure on myself over a long period of time to reproduce the intensity of *Nebraska* on *Born in the U.S.A.* I never got it. But "Born in the U.S.A." is probably one of my five or six best songs, and there was something about the grab-bag nature of the rest of the album that probably made it one of my purest pop records.

Born in the U.S.A. changed my life and gave me my largest audience. It forced me to question the way I presented my music and made me think harder about what I was doing.

An alternate cover shot for *Born in the U.S.A.*

born in the u.s.a.

Born down in a dead man's town
The first kick I took was when I hit the
  ground
You end up like a dog that's been beat
  too much
Till you spend half your life just cover-
  ing up
Born in the U.S.A.
I was born in the U.S.A.
I was born in the U.S.A.
Born in the U.S.A.

Got in a little hometown jam
So they put a rifle in my hand
Sent me off to a foreign land
To go and kill the yellow man

Born in the U.S.A.
I was born in the U.S.A.
I was born in the U.S.A.
I was born in the U.S.A.

Come back home to the refinery
Hiring man says "Son if it was up to
  me"

Went down to see my V.A. man
He said "Son don't you understand
  now"

Had a brother at Khe Sahn fighting off
  the Viet Cong
They're still there, he's all gone
He had a woman he loved in Saigon
I got a picture of him in her arms now

Down in the shadow of the penitentiary
Out by the gas fires of the refinery
I'm ten years burning down the road
Nowhere to run, ain't got nowhere to go

Born in the U.S.A.
I was born in the U.S.A.
Born in the U.S.A.
I'm a long gone daddy in the U.S.A.
Born in the U.S.A.
Born in the U.S.A.
Born in the U.S.A.
I'm a cool rocking daddy in the U.S.A.

cover me

The times are tough now
Just getting tougher
This old world is rough
It's just getting rougher
Cover me
Come on baby cover me
Well I'm looking for a lover who will
    come on in and cover me

Promise me baby you won't
Let them find us
Hold me in your arms
Let's let our love blind us
Cover me
Shut the door and cover me
Well I'm looking for a lover who will
    come on in and cover me

Outside's the rain, the driving snow
I can hear the wild wind blowing
Turn out the light
Bolt the door
I ain't going out there no more
This whole world is out there
Just trying to score
I've seen enough
I don't want to see any more
Cover me
Come on in and cover me
I'm looking for a lover who will come on
    in and cover me

darlington county

Driving into Darlington County
Me and Wayne on the Fourth of July
Driving into Darlington County
Looking for some work on the county
    line
We drove down from New York City
Where the girls are pretty but they just
    want to know your name
Driving into Darlington City
Got a union connection with an uncle of
    Wayne's
We drove eight hundred miles without
    seeing a cop
We got rock and roll music blasting off
    the t-top singing—

CHORUS:
Sha la la
Sha la la la la la
Sha la la la la la la la

Hey little girl standing on the corner
Today's your lucky day for sure all right
Me and my buddy we're from New York
    City
We got two hundred dollars, we want to
    rock all night
Girl, you're looking at two big spenders
Why the world don't know what me and
    Wayne might do
Our pa's each own one of the World
    Trade Centers
For a kiss and a smile I'll give mine all
    to you
Come on baby take a seat on the fender
It's a long night and tell me what else
    were you gonna do
Just me and you, we could sha la la

(CHORUS)

Little girl sitting in the window
Ain't seen my buddy in seven days
County man tells me the same thing
He don't work and he don't get paid
Little girl, you're so young and pretty
Walk with me and you can have your
    way
And we'll leave this Darlington City
For a ride down that Dixie highway

Driving out of Darlington County
My eyes seen the glory of the coming of
    the Lord
Driving out of Darlington County
Seen Wayne handcuffed to the bumper
    of a state trooper's Ford

(CHORUS)

working on the highway

Friday night's pay night, guys fresh out
of work
Talking about the weekend, scrubbing
off the dirt
Some heading home to their families,
some are looking to get hurt
Some going down to Stovell wearing
trouble on their shirts

I work for the county out on 95
All day I hold a red flag and watch the
traffic pass me by
In my head I keep a picture of a pretty
little miss
Someday, mister, I'm gonna lead a
better life than this

CHORUS:
Working on the highway laying down
the blacktop
Working on the highway, all day long I
don't stop

Working on the highway blasting
through the bedrock
Working on the highway
Working on the highway

I met her at a dance down at the union
hall
She was standing with her brothers,
back up against the wall
Sometimes we'd go walking down the
union tracks
One day I looked straight at her and
she looked straight back

(CHORUS)

I saved up my money and I put it all
away
I went to see her daddy but we didn't
have much to say
"Son, can't you see that she's just a
little girl

She don't know nothing about this
cruel, cruel world"

We lit out down to Florida, we got along
all right
One day her brothers came and got her
and they took me in a black and
white
The prosecutor kept the promise that he
made on that day
And the judge got mad and he put me
straight away
I wake up every morning to the work
bell clang
Me and the warden go swinging on the
Charlotte County road gang

(CHORUS)

downbound train

I had a job, I had a girl
I had something going, mister, in this
    world
I got laid off down at the lumberyard
Our love went bad, times got hard
Now I work down at the car wash
Where all it ever does is rain
Don't you feel like you're a rider
On a downbound train

She just said "Joe I gotta go
We had it once, we ain't got it anymore"
She packed her bags, left me behind
She bought a ticket on the Central Line
Nights as I sleep I hear that whistle
    whining
I feel her kiss in the misty rain
And I feel like I'm a rider
On a downbound train

Last night I heard your voice
You were crying, crying, you were so
    alone
You said your love had never died

You were waiting for me at home
Put on my jacket, I ran through the
    woods
I ran till I thought my chest would
    explode
There in the clearing beyond the high-
    way
In the moonlight our wedding house
    shone
I rushed through the yard, I burst
    through the front door
My head pounding hard, up the stairs I
    climbed
The room was dark, our bed was empty
Then I heard that long whistle whine
And I dropped to my knees, hung my
    head and cried

Now I swing a sledgehammer on a rail-
    road gang
Knocking down them cross ties, working
    in the rain
Now don't it feel like you're a rider
On a downbound train

i'm on fire

Hey little girl, is your daddy home
Did he go away and leave you all alone
I got a bad desire
I'm on fire

Tell me now baby is he good to you
Can he do to you the things that I do
I can take you higher
I'm on fire

Sometimes it's like someone took a
    knife, baby, edgy and dull
And cut a six-inch valley through the
    middle of my soul
At night I wake up with my sheets
    soaking wet
And a freight train running through the
    middle of my head
Only you can cool my desire
I'm on fire

no surrender

We busted out of class, had to get away
    from those fools
We learned more from a three-minute
    record, baby, than we ever learned in
    school
Tonight I hear the neighborhood drum-
    mer sound
I can feel my heart begin to pound
You say you're tired and you just want
    to close your eyes
And follow your dreams down

We made a promise we swore we'd
    always remember
No retreat, baby, no surrender
Like soldiers in the winter's night with a
    vow to defend
No retreat, baby, no surrender

Now young faces grow sad and old
And hearts of fire grow cold
We swore blood brothers against the
    wind
Now I'm ready to grow young again
And hear your sister's voice calling us
    home

Across the open yards
Well maybe we could cut some place of
    our own
With these drums and these guitars

CHORUS:
'Cause we made a promise we swore
    we'd always remember
No retreat, baby, no surrender
Blood brothers in the stormy night with
    a vow to defend
No retreat, baby, no surrender

Now on the street tonight the lights
    grow dim
The walls of my room are closing in
There's a war outside still raging
You say it ain't ours anymore to win
I want to sleep beneath peaceful skies
    in my lover's bed
With a wide open country in my eyes
    and these romantic dreams in my
    head

(CHORUS)

bobby jean

Well I came by your house the other day
Your mother said you went away
She said there was nothing that I could
    have done
There was nothing nobody could say
Me and you we've known each other
Ever since we were sixteen
I wished I would have known
I wished I could have called you
Just to say good-bye, Bobby Jean

Now you hung with me when all the
    others
Turned away, turned up their noses
We liked the same music, we liked the
    same bands
We liked the same clothes
We told each other that we were the
    wildest
The wildest things we'd ever seen
Now I wished you would have told me
I wished I could have talked to you

Just to say good-bye, Bobby Jean

Now we went walking in the rain
Talking about the pain that from the
    world we hid
Now there ain't nobody nowhere nohow
Gonna ever understand me the way you
    did

Maybe you'll be out there on that road
    somewhere
In some bus or train traveling along
In some motel room there'll be a radio
    playing
And you'll hear me sing this song
Well if you do you'll know I'm thinking
    of you
And all the miles in between
And I'm just calling one last time
Not to change your mind, but just to
    say I miss you, baby
Good luck, good-bye, Bobby Jean

Overleaf: Born in the U.S.A. photo shoot, basement, Rumson, New Jersey

i'm goin' down

We sit in the car outside your house
I can feel the heat coming 'round
I go to put my arm around you and you
Give me a look like I'm way out of
    bounds
You let out one of your bored sighs
Well lately when I look into your eyes
I'm goin' down

We get dressed up and we go
Out, baby, for the night
We come home early burning, burning
Burning in some firefight
I'm sick and tired of your setting me up
Setting me up just to knock-a, knock-a,
    knock-a me down

I pull you close now, baby
But when we kiss I can feel a doubt
I remember back when we started
My kisses used to turn you inside out
I used to drive you to work in the
    morning
Friday night I'd drive you all around
You used to love to drive me wild
But lately, girl, you get your kicks from
    just driving me down

glory days

I had a friend was a big baseball
 player
Back in high school
He could throw that speedball by you
Make you look like a fool, boy
Saw him the other night at this road-
 side bar
I was walking in and he was walking
 out
We went back inside, sat down, had a
 few drinks but all he kept talking
 about was—

CHORUS:
Glory days, well they'll pass you by
Glory days, in the wink of a young
 girl's eye
Glory days, glory days

There's a girl that lives up the block
Back in school she could turn all the
 boys' heads
Sometimes on a Friday I'll stop by and
 have a few drinks
After she put her kids to bed

Her and her husband Bobby, well, they
 split up
I guess it's two years gone by now
We just sit around talking about the old
 times
She says when she feels like crying she
 starts laughing thinking about—

(CHORUS)

Think I'm going down to the well
 tonight
And I'm going to drink till I get my fill
And I hope when I get old I don't sit
 around thinking about it
But I probably will
Yeah, just sitting back trying to
 recapture
A little of the glory of
But time slips away and leaves you
 with nothing, mister, but boring
 stories of—

(CHORUS)

Glory Days

I had a friend was a big baseball player
       back in high school
he could throw that speedball by you make
       make you look like a fool boy
saw him the other night at this roadside bar
       I was walkin in he was walkin out
we went back inside sat down had a few
       drinks but all he kept talkin
about was

       glory days, well they pass you by
    glory days in the wink of a young girls
      eye   glory days   glory days

theres a girl lives up the block back in school
       she used to turn all the boys heads
Sometimes on a Friday or Saturday I stop
       by & have a few drinks after she's put
  her kids to bed
er and her husband Bobby well they split up
    I guess it's 2 yrs gone by now
talkin bout old times + (just when she feels like cryin
      she starts laughin (thinkin) about

      glory days they'll pass you by
    glory days in the wink of a young mans eyes
      glory days glory days

my old man sits down at the legion hall at the bar and
they sit around talkin 'bout how everybody goin to hell + the way it
    was back in war II
now people got shop on their flag + put us and I guess that was a time
    man that was a time

Fred of my dads   on the line

My old man worked 20 yrs for the company + they
        let him go
Now everywhere he goes lookin for a job they still
        tell him he's to old
I was 9 yrs old when he was layin in them firewalls
        at the Metuchen Ford plant Assembly line
Now he just sits on a stool at the bar down at the
        Legion hall but I can tell from the look on
        his face exactly whats on his mind
                                            over time

        glory days ~~to me~~ gone bad
        glory days he never had
            glory days   glory days

~~Sometimes on a summer night I'll sit~~
~~out in the yard drink the air till~~
~~comes a chill~~
~~And the air will be warm + still~~
And I hope when I get old I dont sit around
        thinkin bout all this stuff but I'll
                probably will
Just sittin back tryin to recapture just a little
                bit of the glory of
time slips away and leaves you with nothing
                but boring stories of
glory days yea they'll pass you by
glory days in the wink of a young girls eye
        glory days glory days

[Sometimes
        + while I'm goin down to the well + I'm gonna drink
        till I get my fill

dancing in the dark

I get up in the evening
And I ain't got nothing to say
I come home in the morning
I go to bed feeling the same way
I ain't nothing but tired
Man, I'm just tired and bored with
myself
Hey there baby, I could use just a little
help

CHORUS:
You can't start a fire
You can't start a fire without a spark
This gun's for hire
Even if we're just dancing in the dark

Message keeps getting clearer
Radio's on and I'm moving 'round the
place

I check my look in the mirror
I wanna change my clothes, my hair,
my face
Man, I ain't getting nowhere
Just living in a dump like this
There's something happening some-
where
Baby I just know that there is

(CHORUS)

You sit around getting older
There's a joke here somewhere and it's
on me
I'll shake this world off my shoulders
Come on, baby, the laugh's on me

Stay on the streets of this town
And they'll be carving you up all right
They say you gotta stay hungry

Hey, baby, I'm just about starving
tonight
I'm dying for some action
I'm sick of sitting 'round here trying to
write this book
I need a love reaction
Come on now, baby, gimme just
one look

You can't start a fire
Sitting 'round crying over a broken
heart
This gun's for hire
Even if we're just dancing in the dark
You can't start a fire
Worrying about your little world falling
apart
This gun's for hire
Even if we're just dancing in the dark

my hometown

I was eight years old and running with
A dime in my hand
Into the bus stop to pick up a paper
For my old man
I'd sit on his lap in that big old Buick
And steer as we drove through town
He'd tousle my hair and say "Son take
    a good look around
This is your hometown"
This is your hometown
This is your hometown
This is your hometown

In '65 tension was running high
At my high school
There was a lot of fights between the
    black and white

There was nothing you could do
Two cars at a light on a Saturday night
In the backseat there was a gun
Words were passed, in a shotgun blast
Troubled times had come
To my hometown
My hometown
My hometown
My hometown

Now Main Street's whitewashed
    windows
And vacant stores
Seems like there ain't nobody
Wants to come down here no more
They're closing down the textile mill
Across the railroad tracks

Foreman says these jobs are going boys
And they ain't coming back
To your hometown
Your hometown
Your hometown
Your hometown

Last night me and Kate we laid in bed
Talking about getting out
Packing up our bags maybe
Heading south
I'm thirty-five, we got a boy
Of our own now
Last night I sat him up behind the
    wheel
And said "Son take a good look around
This is your hometown"

tunnel
of
love

**B**orn in the U.S.A. was followed by *Live 1975-85,* a summary of my live shows with the E Street Band over the preceding ten years. After its release I felt I'd said what I had to say and did what recorded work I could with the band, for the moment.

Trying to keep the kind of success we had with *Born in the U.S.A.* going would have been a losing game. A glance at rock history would tell you as much. Artists with the ability to engage a mass audience are always involved in an inner debate as to whether it's worth it, whether the rewards compensate for the singlemindedness, energy, and exposure necessary to meet the demands of the crowd. Also, I felt that a large audience is, by nature, transient. If you depend on it too much, it may distort what you do and who you are. It can blind you to the deeper resonances of your work and the importance of your most committed listeners. So I created a series of records that ebbed and flowed. This allowed me to speak to a large audience and then

step back with more reflective work. In 1987, with this in mind, I decided to reintroduce myself to my fans as a songwriter.

I set up my recording equipment above my garage in Rumson, New Jersey, and began demoing. I wanted to go back to the intimacy of home recording. I started to write about something I'd never written about in depth before: men and women.

The songs for *Tunnel of Love* came out of a single place in a short period of time. The songs and the record happened very fast. Most of the recording was done over the course of three weeks. The writing was not painful, and though some thought so, not literally autobiographical. Instead, it uncovered an inner life and unresolved feelings that I had carried inside me for a long time. I was thirty-seven years old; I didn't see myself with suitcase in hand, guitar at my side, on the tour bus for the rest of my life. I assumed my audience was moving on, as I was.

The beginnings of *Tunnel of Love* go back to "Stolen Car" from *The River*. The song's character, drifting through the night, first confronts the angels and devils that drive him towards his love and keep him from ever reaching her. That character became the main voice of my new record; he embodied the transition my characters made into confronting the more intimate struggles of adult love.

Musically, *Tunnel of Love* was shaped by my recording process. I cut the songs live to a rhythm track, which provided the stability and the sense of a ticking clock. The passage of time was a subtext of my new stories. My characters were no longer kids. There was the possibility of life passing them by, of the things they needed—love, a home—rushing out the open window of all those cars I'd placed them in.

The center of *Tunnel of Love* is "Brilliant Disguise." Trust is a fragile thing; it requires allowing others to see as much of ourselves as we have the courage to reveal. But you drop one mask and find another behind it, until you begin to doubt your own feelings about who you are. It's the twin issues of love and identity that form the core of *Tunnel of Love*.

"Brilliant Disguise," "Two Faces," "One Step Up," "Cautious Man," all tell the story of men whose inner sense of themselves is in doubt. "Tougher Than the Rest," "All That Heaven Will Allow," "Walk Like a Man," "Valentine's Day" have characters struggling toward some tenuous commitment. Knowing that when you make that stand, the clock starts, and you walk not just at your partner's side, but alongside your own mortal self. You name the things beyond your work that will give your life its context and meaning. You promise to be faithful to them. The struggle to uncover who you are and to reach that moment and hold on to it, along with the destructive desire to leave it in ruins, binds together the songs on *Tunnel of Love*.

For twenty years I'd written about the man on the road. On *Tunnel of Love* that changed, and my music turned to the hopes and fears of the man in the house.

ain't got you

I got the fortunes of heaven in
diamonds and gold
I got all the bonds, baby, that the bank
could hold
I got houses 'cross the country, honey,
end to end
And everybody, buddy, wants to be my
friend
Well I got all the riches, baby, any man
ever knew
But the only thing I ain't got, honey, I
ain't got you

I got a house full of Rembrandt and
priceless art
And all the little girls they wanna tear
me apart
When I walk down the street people
stop and stare
Well you'd think I might be thrilled but
baby I don't care
'Cause I got more good luck, honey,
than old King Farouk
But the only thing I ain't got, baby, I
ain't got you

I got a big diamond watch sittin' on my
wrist
I try to tempt you, baby, but you just
resist
I made a deal with the devil, babe, I
won't deny
Until I got you in my arms I can't be
satisfied

I got a pound of caviar sitting home
on ice
I got a fancy foreign car that rides like
paradise
I got a hundred pretty women knockin'
down my door
And folks wanna kiss me I ain't even
seen before
I been around the world and all across
the seven seas
Been paid a king's ransom for doin'
what comes naturally
But I'm still the biggest fool, honey,
this world ever knew
'Cause the only thing I ain't got, baby, I
ain't got you

tougher than the rest

Well it's Saturday night
You're all dressed up in blue
I been watching you awhile
Maybe you been watching me too
So somebody ran out
Left somebody's heart in a mess
Well if you're looking for love
Honey I'm tougher than the rest

Some girls they want a handsome Dan
Or some good-lookin' Joe, on their arm
Some girls like a sweet-talkin' Romeo
Well 'round here baby
I learned you get what you can get
So if you're rough enough for love
Honey I'm tougher than the rest

The road is dark
And it's a thin thin line

But I want you to know I'll walk it for
    you any time
Maybe your other boyfriends
Couldn't pass the test
Well if you're rough and ready for love
Honey I'm tougher than the rest

Well it ain't no secret
I've been around a time or two
Well I don't know, baby, maybe you've
    been around too
Well there's another dance
All you gotta do is say yes
And if you're rough and ready for love
Honey I'm tougher than the rest
If you're rough enough for love
Baby I'm tougher that the rest

all that heaven will allow

I got a dollar in my pocket
There ain't a cloud up above
I got a picture in a locket
That says baby I love you
Well if you didn't look then, boys
Then fellas don't go lookin' now
Well here she comes a-walkin'
All that heaven will allow

Say hey there Mister Bouncer
Now all I wanna do is dance
But I swear I left my wallet
Back home in my workin' pants
C'mon, Slim, slip me in, man
I'll make it up to you somehow
I can't be late, I got a date
With all that heaven will allow

Rain and storm and dark skies
Well now they don't mean a thing
If you got a girl that loves you
And who wants to wear your ring
So c'mon Mister Trouble
We'll make it through you somehow
We'll fill this house with all the love
All that heaven will allow

Now some may wanna die young, man
Young and gloriously
Get it straight now, mister
Hey buddy that ain't me
'Cause I got something on my mind
That sets me straight and walkin'
    proud
And I want all the time
All that heaven will allow

Tougher Than the Rest

Some girls want a handsome Dan
    or a pretty boy Joe
Always on their arms they need a
    real Valentino
if your lookin for good looks (beauty) ~~let's~~ well I
    ain't gonna win no beauty test
but if your rough enough for love call on my
    I'm tougher than the rest

Some girls say they gotta have themselves
    a real he-man
they want a toy toy Buddy
    or a real Tarzan
if you need Mr Rambo then daddy be
    my guest
but if your rough + ready for love call on me

Some girls need flower + romance every day
    they go
they want a sweet soft talkin sensitive
    Romeo
well it's poetry you need then baby

I gotta confess ✳ (days of youth)
    past   only
    test   proof

    unless
All you got to say is yes

if your rough + ready for a real love

you know baby I been around a time or two

"Tougher Than the Rest"—originally written as a rockabilly song

you all dressed up + baby it's Saturday night
I been watching you awhile + I got something
to say if you think it's alright

gimme a chance baby I'll prove to ya

you gave your heart before + and
nobody proved to proved
but I'm rough + ready ...
line 2 some girls want happy + got
a Romeo
I ain't no Romeo + baby you ain't no Juliet
but if right any for love baby

I know you been hurt a time or two
that's alright + don't care baby, I
been around too
there's one more dance
we got another dance baby + all you gotta
say is yes tonight...

I know you seen me around too

Now your Romeos are all gone + so are my Juliets

I know you've had men to tell you all
the things you want to hear
whisper soft sweet pretty words in your ear
then when the daylight comes they run
+ leave your heart in a mess

I know you been disappointed once or twice

spare parts

Bobby said he'd pull out, Bobby stayed
in
Janey had a baby, it wasn't any sin
They were set to marry on a summer
day
Bobby got scared and he ran away
Jane moved in with her ma out on
Shawnee Lake
She sighed "Ma sometimes my whole
life feels like one big mistake"
She settled in in a back room, time
passed on
Later that winter a son come along

CHORUS:
Spare parts
And broken hearts
Keep the world turnin' around

Now Janey walked that baby across the
floor night after night
But she was a young girl and she
missed the party lights
Meanwhile in South Texas in a dirty oil
patch
Bobby heard 'bout his son bein' born
and swore he wasn't ever goin' back

(CHORUS)

Janey heard about a woman over in
Calverton
Put her baby in the river, let the river
roll on
She looked at her boy in the crib where
he lay
Got down on her knees, cried till she
prayed

Mist was on the water, low run the tide
Janey held her son down at the river
side
Waist deep in the water, how bright the
sun shone
She lifted him in her arms and carried
him home
As he lay sleeping in her bed Janey took
a look around at everything
Went to a drawer in her bureau and got
out her old engagement ring
Took out her wedding dress, tied that
ring up in its sash
Went straight down to the pawnshop,
man, and walked out with some good
cold cash

(CHORUS)

cautious man

Bill Horton was a cautious man of the
  road
He walked lookin' over his shoulder and
  remained faithful to its code
When something caught his eye he'd
  measure his need
And then very carefully he'd proceed

Billy met a young girl in the early days
  of May
It was there in her arms he let his
  cautiousness slip away
In their lovers' twilight as the evening
  sky grew dim
He'd lay back in her arms and laugh at
  what had happened to him

On his right hand Billy'd tattooed the
  word love and on his left hand was
  the word fear
And in which hand he held his fate was
  never clear
Come Indian summer he took his young
  lover for his bride
And with his own hands built her a
  great house down by the river side

Now Billy was an honest man, he
  wanted to do what was right

He worked hard to fill their lives with
  happy days and loving nights
Alone on his knees in the darkness for
  steadiness he'd pray
For he knew in a restless heart the
  seed of betrayal lay

One night Billy awoke from a terrible
  dream callin' his wife's name
She lay breathing beside him in a
  peaceful sleep, a thousand miles
  away
He got dressed in the moonlight and
  down to the highway he strode
When he got there he didn't find
  nothing but road

Billy felt a coldness rise up inside him
  that he couldn't name
Just as the words tattooed 'cross his
  knuckles he knew would always
  remain
At their bedside he brushed the hair
  from his wife's face as the moon
  shone on her skin so white
Filling their room in the beauty of God's
  fallen light

walk like a man

I remember how rough your hand felt on
    mine
On my wedding day
And the tears cried on my shoulder
I couldn't turn away
Well so much has happened to me
That I don't understand
All I can think of is being five years old
        following behind you at the beach
Tracing your footprints in the sand
Trying to walk like a man

By Our Lady of the Roses
We lived in the shadow of the elms
I remember Ma draggin' me and my
        sister up the street to the church
Whenever she heard those wedding
    bells
Well would they ever look so happy
    again
The handsome groom and his bride
As they stepped into that long black
    limousine

For their mystery ride
Well tonight you step away from me
And alone at the altar I stand
And as I watch my bride coming down
    the aisle I pray
For the strength to walk like a man

Well now the years have gone and I've
    grown
From that seed you've sown
But I didn't think there'd be so many
    steps
I'd have to learn on my own
Well I was young and I didn't know
    what to do
When I saw your best steps stolen away
    from you
Now I'll do what I can
I'll walk like a man
And I'll keep on walkin'

From the "Tunnel of Love" video shoot

tunnel
of love

Fat man sitting on a little stool
Takes the money from my hand while
  his eyes take a walk all over you
Hands me two tickets, smiles and
  whispers good luck
Cuddle up, angel, cuddle up, my little
  dove
We'll ride down, baby, into this tunnel
  of love

I can feel the soft silk of your blouse
And them soft thrills in our little fun-
  house
Then the lights go out and it's just the
  three of us
You, me and all that stuff we're so
  scared of
Gotta ride down, baby, into this tunnel
  of love

There's a crazy mirror showing us both
  in 5-D

I'm laughing at you, you're laughing at
  me
There's a room of shadows that gets so
  dark, brother
It's easy for two people to lose each
  other
In this tunnel of love

It ought to be easy, ought to be simple
  enough
Man meets a woman and they fall in
  love
But the house is haunted and the ride
  gets rough
And you've got to learn to live with
  what you can't rise above
If you want to ride on down in through
  this tunnel of love

two faces

I met a girl and we ran away
I swore I'd make her happy every day
And how I made her cry
Two faces have I

Sometimes, mister, I feel sunny and
   wild
Lord I love to see my baby smile
Then dark clouds come rolling by
Two faces have I

One that laughs, one that cries
One says hello, one says good-bye
One does things I don't understand
Makes me feel like half a man

At night I get down on my knees and
   pray
Our love will make that other man go
   away
But he'll never say good-bye
Two face have I

Last night as I kissed you 'neath the
   willow tree
He swore he'd take your love away from
   me
He said our life was just a lie
And two faces have I
Well go ahead and let him try

brilliant disguise

I hold you in my arms
As the band plays
What are those words whispered, baby
Just as you turn away
I saw you last night
Out on the edge of town
I wanna read your mind
To know just what I've got in
This new thing I've found
So tell me what I see
When I look in your eyes
Is that you, baby
Or just a brilliant disguise

I heard somebody call your name
From underneath our willow
I saw something tucked in shame
Underneath your pillow

Well I've tried so hard, baby
But I just can't see
What a woman like you
Is doing with me
So tell me who I see
When I look in your eyes
Is that you, baby
Or just a brilliant disguise

Now look at me, baby
Struggling to do everything right
And then it falls apart
When out go the lights
I'm just a lonely pilgrim
I walk this world in wealth
I wanna know if it's you I don't trust
'Cause I damn sure don't trust myself

Now you play the loving woman
I'll play the faithful man
But just don't look too close
Into the palm of my hand
We stood at the altar
The gypsy swore our future was right
But come the wee wee hours
Well maybe, baby, the gypsy lied
So when you look at me
You better look hard and look twice
Is that me baby
Or just a brilliant disguise

Tonight our bed is cold
I'm lost in the darkness of our love
God have mercy on the man
Who doubts what he's sure of

one step up

Woke up this morning, the house was
    cold
Checked the furnace, she wasn't
    burnin'
Went out and hopped in my old Ford
Hit the engine but she ain't turnin'
We've given each other some hard
    lessons lately
But we ain't learnin'
We're the same sad story, that's a fact
One step up and two steps back

Bird on a wire outside my motel room
But he ain't singin'
Girl in white outside a church in June
But the church bells they ain't ringin'
I'm sittin' here in this bar tonight
But all I'm thinkin' is
I'm the same old story, same old act
One step up and two steps back

It's the same thing night on night

Who's wrong, baby, who's right
Another fight and I slam the door on
Another battle in our dirty little war
When I look at myself I don't see
The man I wanted to be
Somewhere along the line I slipped off
    track
I'm caught movin' one step up and two
    steps back

There's a girl across the bar
I get the message she's sendin'
Mmm, she ain't lookin' too married
And me, well honey, I'm pretending
Last night I dreamed I held you in my
    arms
The music was never ending
We danced as the evening sky faded to
    black
One step up and two steps back

when you're alone

Times were tough, love was not enough
So you said "Sorry Johnny I'm gone gone
    gone"
You said my act was funny
But we both knew what was missing,
    honey
So you lit out on your own
Now that pretty form that you've got,
    baby
Will make sure you get along
But you're gonna find out some day,
    honey

CHORUS:
When you're alone you're alone
When you're alone you're alone
When you're alone you're alone

When you're alone you ain't nothing but
    alone

Now I was young and pretty on the
    mean streets of the city
And I fought to make 'em my home
With just the shirt on my back I left and
    swore I'd never look back
And man I was gone gone gone
But there's things that'll knock you
    down you don't even see coming
And send you crawling like a baby back
    home
You're gonna find out that day, sugar—

(CHORUS)

I knew some day your runnin' would be
    through
And you'd think back on me and you
And your love would be strong
You'd forget all about the bad and think
    only of all the laughs that we had
And you'd wanna come home
Now it ain't hard feelings or nothin',
    sugar
That ain't what's got me singing this
    song
It's just nobody knows, honey, where
    love goes
But when it goes it's gone gone

(CHORUS)

valentine's day

I'm driving a big lazy car rushin' up the
  highway in the dark
I got one hand steady on the wheel and
  one hand's tremblin' over my heart
It's pounding, baby, like it's gonna bust
  right on through
And it ain't gonna stop till I'm alone
  again with you

A friend of mine became a father last
  night
When we spoke in his voice I could hear
  the light
Of the skies and the rivers the timber-
  wolf in the pines
And that great jukebox out on Route 39
They say he travels fastest who travels
  alone
But tonight I miss my girl, mister,
  tonight I miss my home

Is it the sound of the leaves
Left blown by the wayside
That's got me out here on this spooky
  old highway tonight

Is it the cry of the river
With the moonlight shining through
That ain't what scares me, baby
What scares me is losin' you

They say if you die in your dreams you
  really die in your bed
But, honey, last night I dreamed my
  eyes rolled straight back in my head
And God's light came shinin' on
  through
I woke up in the darkness scared and
  breathin' and born anew
It wasn't the cold river bottom I felt
  rushing over me
It wasn't the bitterness of a dream that
  didn't come true
It wasn't the wind in the gray fields I
  felt rushing through my arms
No no baby it was you
So hold me close, honey, say you're
  forever mine
And tell me you'll be my lonely
  valentine

human touch

Go west, young man. On Hollywood Boulevard.

fter *Tunnel of Love* was released in 1987 and I toured in 1988, I spent the next two years doing very little musically. These were the years in which I saw my family come together. We lived in New York for a while, then we moved to California. I always loved the West, since I first drove through with my manager, Tinker, in the early '70s. When I had free time, I'd head for Arizona and drift through the state on a motorcycle. I'd spent some time in California, since my parents had moved there twenty-five years before. I had a younger sister in Los Angeles, and in the early '80s I bought a small bungalow in the Hollywood Hills.

By 1989 Patti and I were looking for a change of scenery and a fresh start. After a stint in New York City, I realized I still craved some open space. In Los Angeles I could still have my cars and motorcycles, be thirty minutes from the mountains, ocean, and desert, meet some new people, and relax amidst the anonymity of a big city.

Human Touch began as an exercise to get myself back into writing and recording. I wrote a variety of music in genres that I had always liked: soul, rock, pop, R&B. The record, once again, took awhile because I was finding my way to the songs. I also worked for the first time with musicians other than the E Street Band. I felt I needed to see what other people brought with them into the studio and how my music would be affected by collaborating with different talents and personalities.

Roy "The Professor" Bittan—born to be wild

One day in LA Roy Bittan played me a couple of pieces of music that he'd written. I liked them and told him I'd be interested in writing lyrics to them. One of them became "Roll of the Dice," the other became "Real World." I had never collaborated with another songwriter on any of my other records. I was looking for something to get me going; Roy was enthusiastic and had good ideas. He soon joined the production team of *Human Touch,* with Jon and Chuck.

The record took shape when Roy and I would play together in my garage apartment and make tapes of song and arrangement ideas I came up with. Then we'd go into the studio and set up what essentially was a two-man band. I would sing and play guitar; Roy would play the keyboards and

With Patti in New Jersey

bass. Together we'd perform to a drum track. The two of us could create an entire band sound live

in the studio. That way we got a good sense of what songs might work, and those were the ideas we

developed. Then musicians would come in and play to what we recorded, or we'd play with them

and record the songs live. Very often we'd do both and pick what worked the best.

Human Touch was another record that evolved slowly. It took awhile for the songs on the

album to shape themselves into a cohesive whole. In "Human Touch," "Soul Driver," and "Real

World," people search to find some emotional contact, some modest communion, some physical

and sexual connection. But to receive what love delivers, they have to surrender themselves to

each other and accept fate. This tension is at the heart of *Human Touch*.

Writers and artists create little worlds and control them. You do that well enough, and you begin to believe you can live in one of them. But the real world doesn't work that way. Love levels the playing field, you can't predict its outcome, and the same rules apply to all. Both *Human Touch* and *Lucky Town* came out of a moment in which to find what I needed, I was going to have to let things go, change, try new things, make mistakes—just live.

At the end of the *Human Touch* album I still felt I needed another song. So I wrote "Living Proof," about the common strength it takes to constitute a family. Children are the "living proof" of our belief in one another, that love is real. They are faith and hope transformed into flesh and blood.

Once I had written "Living Proof," over the next three weeks I wrote and recorded an entirely new record. It was a release from the long process of making *Human Touch*. I set up the home recording equipment and everything came together very quickly, as on *Nebraska* and *Tunnel of Love*. *Lucky Town* had the ease that came with the relaxed writing and recording of its songs.

"Better Days," "Book of Dreams," and "Leap of Faith" were all songs about second chances. The characters return from broken love affairs and self-doubt and find the tempered optimism to take another shot. "Local Hero" takes an ironic look at "the slings and arrows of outrageous fortune," while "Leap of Faith" is a sexually humorous glimpse at love and resilience. "If I Should Fall

Behind" was one of my best songs about the dedication to one another that comes with love. "The Big Muddy" explores human frailty and the morally ambiguous territory that comes with adulthood.

Scenes from the Persian Gulf War and gang warfare in Los Angeles open "Souls of the Departed." In the song, the character's desire to protect the things he loves most from the violent world around him is undeniable. But the underbelly of that impulse, along with economic injustice, is one of the things that has led us to the racially segregated society we live in. The father in "Souls of the Departed" wrestles with his own hypocrises about the choices he has made for his family in contrast to his beliefs.

Lucky Town closes with "My Beautiful Reward." A man searches for something unnameable, then, slipping between life and death, transforms into a bird flying over gray fields with "the cold wind at my back."

Human Touch and *Lucky Town* were both about the blessings and the unanswerable questions that come with adult life, mortality, and human love.

human touch

You and me we were the pretenders
We let it all slip away
In the end what you don't surrender
Well the world just strips away

Girl, ain't no kindness in the face of
  strangers
Ain't gonna find no miracles here
Well you can wait on your blessings, my
  darlin'
But I got a deal for you right here

I ain't lookin' for prayers or pity
I ain't comin' 'round searchin' for a
  crutch
I just want someone to talk to
And a little of that human touch
Just a little of that human touch

Ain't no mercy on the streets of this
  town
Ain't no bread from heavenly skies
Ain't nobody drawin' wine from this
  blood
It's just you and me tonight

Tell me in a world without pity

Do you think what I'm askin's too much
I just want something to hold on to
And a little of that human touch
Just a little of that human touch

Oh girl, that feeling of safety you prize
Well it comes with a hard hard price
You can't shut off the risk and the pain
Without losin' the love that remains
We're all riders on this train

So you been broken and you been hurt
Show me somebody who ain't
Yeah I know I ain't nobody's bargain
But hell a little touch-up
And a little paint . . .

You might need somethin' to hold on to
When all the answers they don't
  amount to much
Somebody that you can just talk to
And a little of that human touch

Baby in a world without pity
Do you think what I'm askin's too much
I just want to feel you in my arms
And share a little of that human touch

soul driver

Rode through forty nights of the
    gospel's rain
Black sky pourin' snakes, frogs
And love in vain
You were down where the river grows
    wider
Baby let me be your soul driver

Well if something in the air feels a little
    unkind
Don't worry darlin'
It'll slip your mind
I'll be your gypsy joker, your shotgun
    rider
Baby let me be your soul driver

Now no one knows which way love's
    wheel turns
Will we hit it rich
Or crash and burn
Does fortune wait or just the black
    hand of fate
This love potion's all we've got
One toast before it's too late

If the angels are unkind or the season
    is dark
Or if in the end
Love just falls apart
Then here's to our destruction
Baby let me be your soul driver

57 channels [and nothin' on]

I bought a bourgeois house in the
   Hollywood hills
With a trunkload of hundred thousand
   dollar bills
Man came by to hook up my cable TV
We settled in for the night my baby
   and me
We switched 'round and 'round till half-
   past dawn
There was 57 channels and nothin' on

Well now home entertainment was my
   baby's wish
So I hopped into town for a satellite
   dish

I tied it to the top of my Japanese car
I came home and I pointed it out into
   the stars
A message came back from the great
   beyond
"There's 57 channels and nothin' on"

Well we might'a made some friends
   with some billionaires
We might'a got all nice and friendly
If we'd made it upstairs
All I got was a note that said "Bye-bye
   John
Our love is 57 channels and nothin' on"

So I bought a .44 Magnum, it was solid
   steel cast
And in the blessed name of Elvis, well I
   just let it blast
Till my TV lay in pieces there at my feet
And they busted me for disturbin' the
   almighty peace
Judge said "What you got in your
   defense, son?"
57 channels and nothin' on
I can see by your eyes, friend, you're
   just about gone
57 channels and nothin' on
57 channels and nothin' on

cross my heart

First time I crossed my heart
I was beggin' baby please
At your bedside down on my knees
When I crossed my heart
When I crossed my heart
I crossed my heart, pretty baby over you

Second time I crossed my heart
Rain came in from the south
I was lyin' there with something sweet
    and salty in my mouth
When I crossed my heart
When I crossed my heart
When I crossed my heart, pretty darlin'
    over you

Well you may think the world's black
    and white
And you're dirty or you're clean
You better watch out you don't slip
Through them spaces in between

Where the night gets sticky
And the sky gets black

I grabbed you, baby, you grabbed me
    back
And we crossed our hearts
We crossed our hearts
Yeah I crossed my heart

Little boys little girls
They know their wrongs from their
    rights
Once you cross your heart
We crossed our hearts
You ain't ever supposed to lie

Well life ain't nothin'
But a cold hard ride
I ain't leavin'
Till I'm satisfied
I cross my heart
Yeah I cross my heart
Well I cross my heart, pretty darlin'
    over you

gloria's eyes

I was your big man, I was your Prince
   Charming
King on a white horse, hey now look
   how far I've fallen
I tried to trick you, yeah, but baby you
   got wise
You cut me, cut me right down to size
Now I'm just a fool in Gloria's eyes

Swore I'd get you back I was so sure
I'd get you back like I done so many
   times before
A little sweet talk to cover over all of
   the lies
You came runnin' back but to my
   surprise
There was somethin' gone in Gloria's
   eyes

Well in the dark when it was just me
   and you

I asked the question that I knew the
   answer to
Is that a smile, my little dolly, on the
   shelf
Tell me is that a smile
Or is it somethin' else

Now I work hard to prove my love is
   true
Now I work hard and I bring it on home
   to you
At night I pray as silently you lie
Some day my love again will rise
Like a shining torch in Gloria's eyes

I was your big man, your Prince
   Charming
King on a white horse, now look how far
   I've fallen

with every wish

Ol' catfish in the lake we called him
  Big Jim
When I was a kid my only wish was to
  get my line in him
Skipped church one Sunday, rowed out
  and throw'd in my line
Jim took that hook, pole and me right
  over the side
Went driftin' down past old tires and
  rusty cans of beer
The angel of the lake whispered in
  my ear
"Before you choose your wish, son
You better think first
With every wish there comes a curse"

I fell in love with beautiful Doreen
She was the prettiest thing this old
  town'd ever seen
I courted her and I made her mine
But I grew jealous whenever another
  man'd come walkin' down the line
And my jealousy made me treat her
  mean and cruel
She sighed "Bobby, oh Bobby, you're
  such a fool

Don't you know before you choose your
  wish
You'd better think first
'Cause with every wish there comes a
  curse"

These days I sit around and laugh
At the many rivers I've crossed
But on the far banks there's always
  another forest
Where a man can get lost
Well there in the high trees love's
  bluebird glides
Guiding us 'cross to another river on
  the other side
And there someone is waitin' with a
  look in her eyes
And though my heart's grown weary
And more than a little bit shy
Tonight I'll drink from her waters to
  quench my thirst
And leave the angels to worry
With every wish

Gloria's Eyes

Once I was a big man
darlin (baby) I was your prince charmin'
A king on a white horse

    oh baby how far I've fallen
I did something stupid, and baby you got wise
you cut me baby cut me right down
    to size   now I'm just a fool
  in Gloria's eyes

is I   door
and I'd guess I smoothly talk you
and I'd win your heart back over like I'd so many
    times before
something was different   (As the stars prophesized
  oh yeah you gave in but soon I realized
(and soon yes you came back)
    something had changed + took the shine
    off my prize
for when I held you close I couldn't
  stand what I saw

And that's my love your words never repeated
  what was it I saw I saw reflected
    in Glo...

so now I work hard and boy is all I have to ya
  that will enough darlin that I could do
    for you
I sweat & slave until once I claim my
  prize
    one day until once my love shall
    again I rise
  in Gloria's eyes

was that a smile   shelf
was that a smile or was it
            something else?

                    + swear you the only one
+ each night I caress you ~~~~ run my
figures thru your hair
searching + searing for the light that comes never
            there but
~~~vain~~
searching in ~~~~ vain for the answer that
so I hold the question never comes
        so I'll sweat + slave until the day arrives
        when once again find my love will rise
                in Glass eyes

roll of the dice

Well I've been a losin' gambler
Just throwin' snake eyes
Love ain't got me downhearted
I know up around the corner lies
My fool's paradise
In just another roll of the dice

All my elevens and sevens been comin'
    up
Sixes and nines
But since I fell for you baby
Been comin' on changin' times
They're waitin' over the rise
Just another roll of the dice

I've stumbled and I know I made my
    mistakes
But tonight I'm gonna be playin' for all
    of the stakes

Well it's never too late, so come on girl

The tables are waiting
You and me and lady luck, well, tonight
We'll be celebrating
Drinkin' champagne on ice
In just another roll of the dice

High rollers lay down your bets and I'll
    raise 'em
Well I know the odds ain't in my favor

Maybe I'm just a clown throwin' down
Lookin' to come up busted
I'm a thief in the house of love
And I can't be trusted
Well I'll be makin' my heist
In just another roll of the dice
Just another roll of the dice
Move on up
Come on seven
Roll me baby
In this fool's heaven

real world

Mister Trouble come walkin' this way
Year gone past feels like one long day
But I'm alive and I'm feelin' all right
Well I run that hard road outta heart-
    break city
Built a roadside carnival out of hurt
    and self-pity
It was all wrong, well now I'm movin'
    on

Ain't no church bells ringing
Ain't no flags unfurled
Just me and you and the love we're
    bringing
Into the real world
Into the real world

I built a shrine in my heart, it wasn't
    pretty to see
Made out of fool's gold, memory and
    tears cried
Now I'm headin' over the rise
I'm searchin' for one clear moment of
    love and truth

I still got a little faith
But what I need is some proof tonight
I'm lookin' for it in your eyes

Ain't no church bells ringing
Ain't no flags unfurled
Just me and you and the love we're
    bringing
Into the real world
Into the real world

Well tonight I just wanna shout
I feel my soul waist deep and sinkin'
Into this black river of doubt
I just wanna rise and walk along the
    river side
And when the morning comes, baby, I
    don't wanna hide
I'll stand right at your side with my
    arms open wide

Well tonight I just wanna shout
I feel my soul waist deep and sinkin'
Into this black river of doubt

I just wanna rise and walk along the
    river side
Till the morning comes
I'll stand right by your side

I wanna find some answers, I wanna
    ask for some help
I'm tired of runnin' scared
Baby let's get our bags packed
We'll take it here to hell and heaven
    and back
And if love is hopeless, hopeless at best
Come on put on your party dress, it's
    ours tonight
And we're goin' with the tumblin' dice

Ain't no church bells ringing
Ain't no flags unfurled
Just me, you and the hope we're
    bringing
Into the real world
Well into the real world
Oh into the real world

all or nothin' at all

Said you'd give me just a little kiss
And you'd rock me for a little while
Well you'd slip me just a piece of it
Listen up my little child
I want it all or nothin' at all
I want it all or nothin' at all

Said you'd take me for a little dance
If you had a little time on your hands
Well all I do is push and shove
Just to get a little piece of your love
I want it all or nothin' at all
I want it all or nothin' at all

Well now I don't wanna be greedy
But when it comes to love there ain't no
   doubt

You just ain't gonna get what you want
With one foot in bed and one foot out
You got to give it all or nothin' at all
All or nothin' at all

Now I only got a little time
So if you're gonna change your mind
Then shout out what you're thinkin' of
If what you're thinkin' of is love
I want it all or nothin' at all
I want it all or nothin' at all
I want to have it all or nothin' at all
I want it all or nothin' at all

I want it all or nothin' at all
I want to give it all or nothin' at all

man's job

Well you can go out with him
Play with all of his toys
But takin' care of you darlin'
Ain't for one of the boys
Oh there's somethin' in your soul
That he's gonna rob
And lovin' you baby, lovin' you darlin'
Lovin' you woman is a man's man's job

CHORUS:
Lovin' you is a man's job baby
Lovin' you is a man's job
Lovin' you is a man's job baby
Lovin' you is a man's job

Well now his kisses may thrill

Those other girls that he likes
But when it comes to treatin'
A real woman right
Well all of his tricks
No they won't be enough
'Cause lovin' you baby, lovin' you
     woman
Lovin' you darlin' is a man's man's job

(CHORUS)

You're dancin' with him, he's holding
     you tight
I'm standing here waitin' to catch your
     eye

Your hand's on his neck as the music
     sways
All my illusions slip away

Now if you're lookin' for a hero
Someone to save the day
Well darlin' my feet
They're made of clay
But I've got somethin' in my soul
And I wanna give it up
But gettin' up the nerve
Gettin' up the nerve
Gettin' up the nerve is a man's
     man's job

(CHORUS)

i wish i were blind

I love to see the cottonwood blossom
In the early spring
I love to see the message of love
That the bluebird brings
But when I see you walkin' with him
Down along the strand
I wish I were blind
When I see you with your man

I love to see your hair shining
In the long summer's light
I love to watch the stars fill the sky
On a summer night
The music plays, you take his hand
I watch how you touch him as you start
   to dance
And I wish I were blind

When I see you with your man

We struggle here but all our love's in
   vain
Oh these eyes that once filled me with
   your beauty
Now fill me with pain
And the light that once entered here
Is banished from me
And this darkness is all, baby, that my
   heart sees

And though this world is filled
With a grace and beauty of God's hand
Oh I wish I were blind
When I see you with your man

the long goodbye

My soul went walkin' but I stayed here
Feel like I been workin' for a thousand
   years
Chippin' away at this chain of my own
   lies
Climbin' a wall a hundred miles high
Well I woke up this morning on the
   other side
Yeah yeah this is the long goodbye
Hey yeah this is the long goodbye

Same old faces, it's the same old town
What once was laughs is draggin' me
   now
Waitin' on rain hangin' on for love
Words of forgiveness from some God
   above
Ain't no words of mercy comin' from on
   high
Oh no just a long goodbye

Well I went to leave twenty years ago
Since then I guess I been packin' kinda
   slow
Sure did like that admirin' touch
Guess I liked it a little too much

The moon is high and here I am
Sittin' here with this hammer in hand
One more drink oughtta ease the pain
Starin' at that last link in the chain
Well let's raise our glass and let the
   hammer fly
Hey yeah this is the long goodbye
Hey yeah this is the long goodbye
Kiss me baby and we're gonna fly
Hey yeah this is the long goodbye
Yeah yeah this is the long goodbye
Hey yeah this is the long goodbye
Kiss me baby 'cause we're gonna ride
Yeah yeah this is the long goodbye

r e a l   m a n

Took my baby to a picture show
Found a seat in the back row
Sound came up, lights went down
Rambo he was blowin' 'em down
I don't need no gun in my fist, baby
All I need is your sweet kiss
To get me feelin' like a real man
Feelin' like a real man
Well you can beat on your chest
Hell any monkey can
But you got me feelin' like a real man
Oh feelin' like a real man

Me and my girl Saturday night
Late movie on channel five
The girls were droppin', they're droppin'
    like flies
To some smooth-talkin' cool walkin'
    private eye
I ain't got no nerves of steel
But all I got to know is if your love
    is real
To get me feelin' like a real man
Oh feelin' like a real man
Well you can beat on your chest
Hell any monkey can
Your love's got me feelin' like a real
    man
Oh feelin' like a real man

I ain't no fighter, that's easy to see
And as a lover I ain't goin' down in
    history
But when the lights go down and you
    pull me close
Well I look in your eyes and there's one
    thing I know
Baby I'll be tough enough
If I can find the guts to give you all
    my love
Then I'll be feelin' like a real man
Feelin' like a real man
Well you can beat on your chest
Hell any monkey can
You got me feelin' like a real man
Oh feelin' like a real man
Yeah I been feelin' like a real man
Feelin' like a real man

lucky town

The video shoot for "Better Days"

better days

Well my soul checked out missing as I
  sat listening
To the hours and minutes tickin' away
Yeah just sittin' around waitin' for my
  life to begin
While it was all just slippin' away
I'm tired of waitin' for tomorrow to
  come
Or that train to come roarin' 'round the
  bend
I got a new suit of clothes and a pretty
  red rose
And a woman I can call my friend

These are better days, baby
Yeah there's better days shining
  through
These are better days, baby
Better days with a girl like you

Well I took a piss at fortune's sweet kiss
It's like eatin' caviar and dirt
It's a sad funny ending to find yourself
  pretending
A rich man in a poor man's shirt
Now my ass was draggin' when from a
  passin' gypsy wagon
Your heart like a diamond shone
Tonight I'm layin' in your arms carvin'
  lucky charms
Out of these hard luck bones

These are better days, baby
These are better days it's true
These are better days, baby
There's better days shining through

Now a life of leisure and a pirate's
  treasure
Don't make much for tragedy

But it's a sad man, my friend, who's
  livin' in his own skin
And can't stand the company
Every fool's got a reason for feelin' sorry
  for himself
And turning his heart to stone
Tonight this fool's halfway to heaven
  and just a mile outta hell
And I feel like I'm comin' home

These are better days, baby
There's better days shining through
These are better days
Better days with a girl like you

These are better days, baby
These are better days it's true
These are better days
Better days are shining through

l u c k y   t o w n

House got too crowded, clothes got too
tight
And I don't know just where I'm going
tonight
Out where the sky's been cleared by a
good hard rain
There's somebody callin' my secret
name

I'm going down to Lucky Town
Going down to Lucky Town
I wanna lose these blues I've found
Down in Lucky Town
Down in Lucky Town

Had a coat of fine leather and snakeskin boots
But that coat always had a thread
hangin' loose
Well I pulled it one night and to my
surprise
It led me right past your house and on
over the rise

I'm going down to Lucky Town
Down to Lucky Town

I wanna lose these blues I've found
Down in Lucky Town
Down in Lucky Town

I had some victory that was just failure
in deceit
Now the joke's comin' up through the
soles of my feet
I been a long time walking on fortune's
cane
Tonight I'm steppin' lightly and feelin'
no pain

Well here's to your good looks, baby,
now here's to my health
Here's to the loaded places that we take
ourselves
When it comes to luck you make your
own
Tonight I got dirt on my hands but I'm
building me a new home

Down in Lucky Town
Down in Lucky Town
I'm gonna lose these blues I've found
Down in Lucky Town

With good friend and road buddy Matt DiLea on Route 66, Arizona

local hero

I was driving through my hometown
I was just kinda killin' time
When I seen a face staring out of a
    black velvet painting
From the window of the five-and-dime
I couldn't quite recall the name
But the pose looked familiar to me
So I asked the salesgirl "Who was that
    man
Between the Doberman and Bruce Lee?"
She said "Just a local hero
Local hero" she said with a smile
"Yeah a local hero
He used to live here for a while"

I met a stranger dressed in black
At the train station
He said "Son your soul can be saved"
There's beautiful women, nights of low
    livin'

And some dangerous money to be made
There's a big town 'cross the whiskey
    line
And if we turn the right cards up
They make us boss, the devil pays off
And them folks that are real hard up
They get their local hero
Somebody with the right style
They get their local hero
Somebody with just the right smile

Well I learned my job, I learned it well
Fit myself with religion and a story to
    tell
First they made me the king, then they
    made me pope
Then they brought the rope

I woke to a gypsy girl sayin' "Drink this"

Well my hands had lost all sensation
These days I'm feeling all right
'Cept I can't tell my courage from my
    desperation
From the tainted chalice
Well I drunk some heady wine
Tonight I'm layin' here
But there's something in my ear
Sayin' there's a little town just beneath
    the floodline
Needs a local hero
Somebody with the right style
Lookin' for a local hero
Somebody with the right smile
"Local hero, local hero" she said with a
    smile
Local hero, he used to live here for a
    while

Overleaf: With the hardest-working dog in show business. *Lucky Town* photo shoot.

if i should fall behind

We said we'd walk together, baby come
what may
That come the twilight should we lose
our way
If as we're walking a hand should slip
free
I'll wait for you
And if I should fall behind
Wait for me

We swore we'd travel, darlin' side by
side
We'd help each other stay in stride
But each lover's steps fall so differently
But I'll wait for you
And if I should fall behind
Wait for me

Now everyone dreams of a love lasting
and true

But you and I know what this world
can do
So let's make our steps clear that the
other may see
And I'll wait for you
If I should fall behind
Wait for me

Now there's a beautiful river in the
valley ahead
There 'neath the oak's bough soon we
will be wed
Should we lose each other in the
shadow of the evening trees
I'll wait for you
And should I fall behind
Wait for me
Darlin' I'll wait for you
Should I fall behind
Wait for me

leap of faith

All over the world the rain was pourin'
I was scratchin' where it itched
Oh heartbreak and despair got nothing
   but boring
So I grabbed you baby like a wild pitch

CHORUS:
It takes a leap of faith to get things
   going
It takes a leap of faith, you gotta show
   some guts
It takes a leap of faith to get things
   going
In your heart you must trust

Now your legs were heaven, your
   breasts were the altar
Your body was the holy land
You shouted "jump" but my heart
   faltered
You laughed and said "Baby don't you
   understand?"

(CHORUS)

Now you were the Red Sea, I was Moses
I kissed you and slipped into a bed of
   roses

The waters parted and love rushed
   inside
I was Jesus' son sanctified

Tonight the moon's looking young but
   I'm feelin' younger
'Neath a veil of dreams sweet blessings
   rain
Honey I can feel the first breeze of
   summer
And in your love I'm born again

(CHORUS)

the big muddy

Billy had a mistress down on A and
    Twelfth
She was that little somethin' that he did
    for himself
His own little secret didn't hurt nobody
Come the afternoon he'd take her wadin'

CHORUS:
Waist deep in the big muddy
Waist deep in the big muddy
You start out standing but end up
    crawlin'

Got in some trouble and needed a hand
    from a friend of mine
This old friend he had a figure in mind
It was nothing illegal, just a little bit
    funny
He said "C'mon don't tell me that the
    rich don't know
Sooner or later it all comes down to
    money"
And you're waist deep in the big muddy

Waist deep in the big muddy
You start on higher ground but end up
    crawlin'

Well I had a friend said "You watch
    what you do
Poison snake bites you and you're
    poison too"

How beautiful the river flows and the
    birds they sing
But you and I we're messier things
There ain't no one leavin' this world,
    buddy
Without their shirttail dirty or their
    hands bloody

Waist deep in the big muddy
Waist deep in the big muddy
You start on higher ground but end up
    somehow crawlin'
Waist deep in the big muddy

living proof

Well now on a summer night in a dusky
    room
Come a little piece of the Lord's undying
    light
Crying like he swallowed the fiery moon
In his mother's arms it was all the
    beauty I could take
Like the mission words to some prayer
    that I could never make
In a world so hard and dirty, so fouled
    and confused
Searching for a little bit of God's mercy
I found living proof

I put my heart and soul, I put 'em high
    up on a shelf
Right next to the faith, the faith that I'd
    lost in myself

I went down into the desert city
Just tryin' so hard to shed my skin
I crawled deep into some kind of
    darkness
Lookin' to burn out every trace of who
    I'd been
You do some sad sad things, baby
When it's you you're tryin' to lose
You do some sad and hurtful things
I've seen living proof

You shot through my anger and rage
To show me my prison was just an open
    cage
There were no keys, no guards
Just one frightened man and some old
    shadows for bars

Well now all that's sure on the
    boulevard
Is that life is just a house of cards
As fragile as each and every breath
Of this boy sleepin' in our bed
Tonight let's lie beneath the eaves
Just a close band of happy thieves
And when that train comes we'll get on
    board
And steal what we can from the
    treasures, treasures of the Lord
It's been a long long drought, baby
Tonight the rain's pourin' down on
    our roof
Looking for a little bit of God's mercy
I found living proof

book of dreams

I'm standing in the backyard
Listening to the party inside
Tonight I'm drinkin' in the forgiveness
This life provides
The scars we carry remain but the pain
  slips away it seems
Oh won't you, baby, be in my book of
  dreams

I'm watchin' you through the window
With your girlfriends from back home
You're showin' off your dress
There's laughter and a toast
From your daddy to the prettiest bride
  he's ever seen
Oh won't you, baby, be in my book of
  dreams

In the darkness my fingers slip across
  your skin

I feel your sweet reply
The room fades away and suddenly I'm
  way up high
Just holdin' you to me
As through the window the moonlight
  streams
Oh won't you, baby, be in my book of
  dreams

Now the ritual begins
'Neath the wedding garland we meet as
  strangers
The dance floor is alive with beauty
Mystery and danger
We dance out 'neath the stars' ancient
  light into the darkening trees
Oh won't you, baby, be in my book of
  dreams

souls of
the departed

On the road to Basra stood young
    Lieutenant Jimmy Bly
Detailed to go through the clothes of
    the soldiers who died
At night in dreams he sees their souls
    rise
Like dark geese into the Oklahoma skies

Well this is a prayer for the souls of the
    departed
Those who've gone and left their babies
    brokenhearted
This is a prayer for the souls of the
    departed

Now Raphael Rodriquez was just seven
    years old
Shot down in a schoolyard by some East
    Compton *cholos*
His mama cried "My beautiful boy is
    dead"
In the hills the self-made men just
    sighed and shook their heads

This is a prayer for the souls of the
    departed
Those who've gone and left their babies
    brokenhearted
Young lives over before they got started
This is a prayer for the souls of the
    departed

Tonight as I tuck my own son in bed
All I can think of is what if it would've
    been him instead
I want to build me a wall so high
    nothing can burn it down
Right here on my own piece of dirty
    ground

Now I ply my trade in the land of king
    dollar
Where you get paid and your silence
    passes as honor
And all the hatred and dirty little lies
Been written off the books and into
    decent men's eyes

my beautiful reward

Well I sought gold and diamond rings
My own drug to ease the pain that
    living brings
Walked from the mountain to the valley
    floor
Searching for my beautiful reward
Searching for my beautiful reward

From a house on a hill a sacred light
    shines
I walk through these rooms but none of
    them are mine
Down empty hallways I went from door
    to door
Searching for my beautiful reward
Searching for my beautiful reward

Well your hair shone in the sun
I was so high I was the lucky one
Then I came crashing down like a drunk
    on a barroom floor
Searching for my beautiful reward
Searching for my beautiful reward

Tonight I can feel the cold wind at my
    back
I'm flyin' high over gray fields, my
    feathers long and black
Down along the river's silent edge I soar
Searching for my beautiful reward
Searching for my beautiful reward

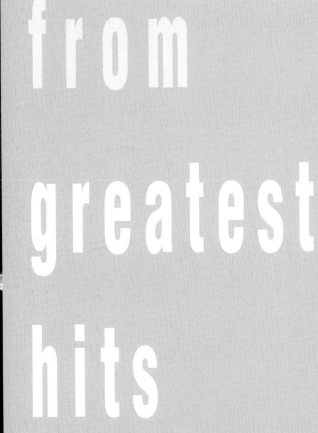

from

greatest

hits

streets of philadelphia

secret garden

murder incorporated

blood brothers

this hard land

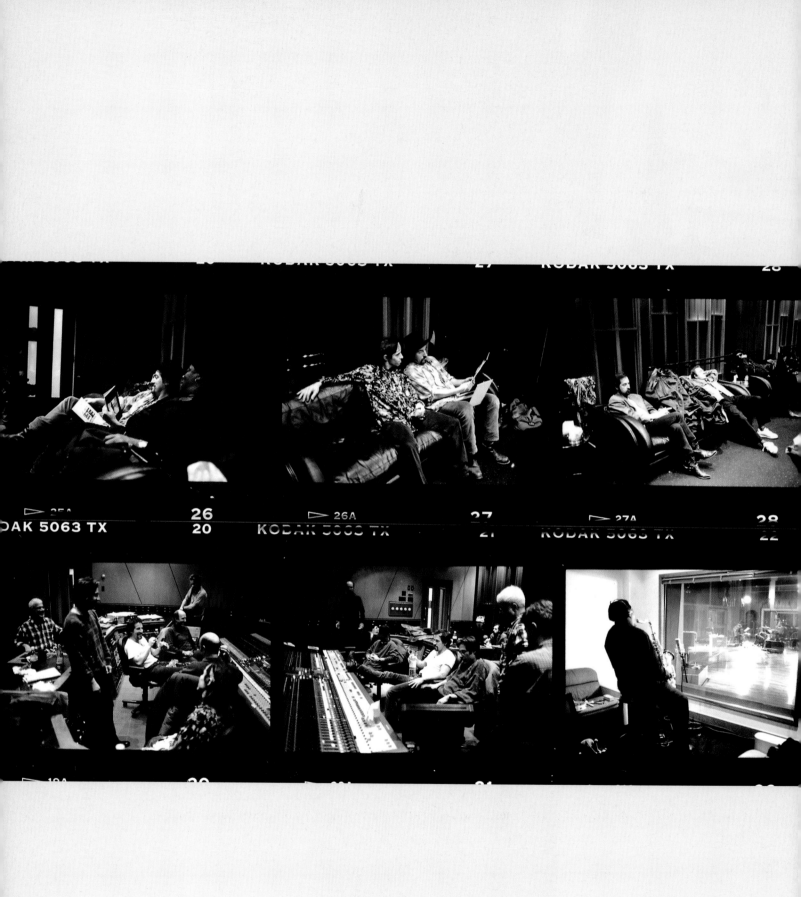

One afternoon in 1994 I received a phone call from Jonathan Demme. We'd met a few years earlier on a video shoot. Jonathan was calling to ask if I'd consider writing a song for a film he was currently directing called *Philadelphia*. The film was about a gay man's battle with AIDS and the fight to retain his position at a prestigious Philadelphia law firm.

I had my studio set up at home in Rumson and for a few afternoons I went in with some lyrics I had partially written dealing with the death of a close friend. Jonathan requested a rock song to open the film. I spent a day or so trying to accommodate, but the lyrics I had seemed to resist being put to rock music. So I began to fiddle with the synthesizer, playing over a hip-hop-influenced beat I programmed on the drum machine. As soon as I slowed the rhythm down over some basic minor chords, the lyrics fell into place and the voice I was looking for came forward.

I finished the song in a few hours and sent the tape off to Jonathan, figuring I hadn't gotten it, but to see if he had a use for it anyway. He phoned me in a few days saying he loved it and placed it over the images of the city of Philadelphia at the top of the film

"Streets of Philadelphia" was a hit because of the film and because it addressed something that the country was attempting to come to grips with at that moment. How do we treat our sons and daughters confronting AIDS? How do we provide them the acceptance and compassion that overcomes prejudice and ties disparate communities together?

"Murder Incorporated" was an outtake from *Born in the U.S.A.* It dealt with the paranoia and compounded violence of life in America. Gated communities, the loss of freedom, and the mistrust of your own neighbor are the price we pay for writing off generations of young people to poverty, drug dependency, and severely limited hopes and dreams.

"Secret Garden" was a cut from an unreleased album I recorded in 1994. It was darkly erotic and centered around the mysteries that remain between partners, even in the closest of relationships.

I wrote "Blood Brothers" on the eve of recording with the E Street Band again. The song is filled with the ambivalence and deep affection of revisiting a relationship spanning twenty-five plus years. You hope the rough spots are balanced out by your common history, the unique experience you shared, and the love you have for one another. We walked into the Hit Factory, got behind our instruments, and had a great time.

"This Hard Land" traces the search for "home" against the restlessness and isolation that is at the heart of the American character. It's about friendship and survival and ends the album with a shot of idealism.

streets of philadelphia

I was bruised and battered and I
   couldn't tell what I felt
I was unrecognizable to myself
I saw my reflection in a window
I didn't know my own face
Oh brother are you gonna leave me
   wastin' away
On the streets of Philadelphia

I walked the avenue till my legs felt like
   stone
I heard the voices of friends vanished
   and gone
At night I could hear the blood in my
   veins
Black and whispering as the rain

On the streets of Philadelphia

Ain't no angel gonna greet me
It's just you and I, my friend
My clothes don't fit me no more
I walked a thousand miles
Just to slip this skin

The night has fallen, I'm lyin' awake
I can feel myself fading away
So receive me, brother, with your
   faithless kiss
Or will we leave each other alone like
   this
On the streets of Philadelphia

secret garden

She'll let you in her house
If you come knockin' late at night
She'll let you in her mouth
If the words you say are right
If you pay the price
She'll let you deep inside
But there's a secret garden she hides

She'll let you in her car
To go drivin' 'round
She'll let you into the parts of herself
That'll bring you down
She'll let you in her heart
If you got a hammer and a vise
But into her secret garden, don't think
   twice

You've gone a million miles
How far'd you get
To that place where you can't remember
And you can't forget

She'll lead you down a path
There'll be tenderness in the air
She'll let you come just far enough
So you know she's really there
She'll look at you and smile
And her eyes will say
She's got a secret garden
Where everything you want
Where everything you need
Will always stay
A million miles away

murder incorporated

Bobby's got a gun that he keeps
   beneath his pillow
Out on the street your chances are zero
Take a look around you (come on now)
It ain't too complicated
You're messin' with Murder
   Incorporated

Now you check over your shoulder
   everywhere that you go
Walkin' down the street there's eyes in
   every shadow
You better take a look around you (come
   on now)
That equipment you got's so outdated
You can't compete with Murder
   Incorporated
Everywhere you look now, Murder
   Incorporated

So you keep a little secret deep down
   inside your dresser drawer
For dealing with the heat you're feelin'
   out on the killin' floor

No matter where you step you feel
   you're never out of danger
So the comfort that you keep's a gold-
   plated snub-nose .32
I heard that you
Got a job downtown man that leaves
   your head cold
Everywhere you look life's ain't got
   no soul
That apartment you live in feels like it's
   just a place to hide
When you're walkin' down the street you
   won't meet no one eye to eye
The cops reported you as just another
   homicide
But I can tell that you were just
   frustrated
From living with Murder Incorporated
Everywhere you look now, Murder
   Incorporated
Murder Incorporated

blood brothers

We played the King of the Mountain out
on the end
The world came chargin' up the hill and
we were women and men
Now there's so much that time, time
and memory fade away
We got our own roads to ride and
chances we gotta take
We stood side by side each one fightin'
for the other
We said until we died we'd always be
blood brothers

Now the hardness of this world slowly
grinds your dreams away
Makin' a fool's joke out of the promises
we make
And what once seemed black and white
turns to so many shades of gray
We lose ourselves in work to do and
bills to pay
And it's a ride, ride, ride, and there
ain't much cover

With no one runnin' by your side, my
blood brother

On through the houses of the dead past
those fallen in their tracks
Always movin' ahead and never lookin'
back
Now I don't know how I feel, I don't
know how I feel tonight
If I've fallen 'neath the wheel, if I've
lost or I've gained sight
I don't even know why, I don't know why
I made this call
Or if any of this matters anymore
after all

But the stars are burnin' bright like
some mystery uncovered
I'll keep movin' through the dark with
you in my heart
My blood brother

this hard land

Hey there mister can you tell me what
    happened to the seeds I've sown
Can you give me a reason, sir, as to
    why they've never grown
They've just blown around from town to
    town
Till they're back out on these fields
Where they fall from my hand
Back into the dirt of this hard land

Now me and my sister from German-
    town
We did ride
We made our bed, sir, from the rock on
    the mountainside
We been blowin' around from town to
    town
Lookin' for a place to stand
Where the sun burst through the cloud
To fall like a circle
Like a circle of fire down on this hard
    land

Now even the rain it don't come 'round
It don't come 'round here no more
And the only sound at night's the wind
Slammin' the back porch door
It just stirs you up like it wants to blow
    you down
Twistin' and churnin' up the sand
Leavin' all them scarecrows lyin' face-
    down
Facedown in the dirt of this hard land

From a building up on the hill
I can hear a tape deck blastin' "Home
    on the Range"
I can see them Bar-M choppers
Sweepin' low across the plains
It's me and you, Frank, we're lookin' for
    lost cattle
Our hooves twistin' and churnin' up the
    sand

We're ridin' in the whirlwind searchin'
    for lost treasure
Way down south of the Rio Grande
We're ridin' 'cross that river
In the moonlight
Up onto the banks of this hard land

Hey, Frank, won't you pack your bags
And meet me tonight down at Liberty
    Hall
Just one kiss from you, my brother
And we'll ride until we fall
We'll sleep in the fields
We'll sleep by the rivers and in the
    morning
We'll make a plan
Well if you can make it
Stay hard, stay hungry, stay alive
If you can
And meet me in a dream of this hard
    land

the ghost of tom joad

Recording *Tom Joad* in California

he Ghost of Tom Joad" was among the songs I wrote for the E Street Band to complete the *Greatest Hits* album. It started out as a rock song. But it didn't feel right, so I set it aside. I returned to it some months later, while still unsure of what I wanted to work on next. After working with the band in New York, I went back to California and started recording at home. I had "Straight Time," "Highway 29," and "The Ghost of Tom Joad." I also had a notebook filled with unfinished song ideas.

I began recording with just myself and my acoustic guitar. When I felt I had some workable material, I put together a small, five-piece group. Once I cut "Tom Joad," I had a feeling for the record I wanted to make. It was an acoustic album where I picked up elements of the themes I had worked on in the past and set the stories in the mid-'90s.

As with *Nebraska,* on "Tom Joad" and the songs that followed, the music was minimal; the melodies were uncomplicated, yet played an important role in the storytelling process. The simplicity and plainness, the austere rhythms defined who these characters were and how they expressed themselves.

The precision of the storytelling in these types of songs is very important. The correct detail can speak volumes about who your character is, while the wrong one can shred the credibility of your story. When you get the music and lyrics right in these songs, your voice disappears into the voices of those you've chosen to write about. Basically, I find the characters and listen to them. That always leads to a series of questions about their behavior: What would they do? What would they never do? You try to locate the rhythm of their speech and the nature of their expression.

But all the telling detail in the world doesn't matter if the song lacks an emotional center. That's something you have to pull out of yourself from the commonality you feel with the man or woman you're writing about. By pulling these elements together as well as you can, you shed light on their lives and respect their experiences.

On *Tom Joad* one song led to another. The ex-con of "Straight Time" became the shoe salesman of "Highway 29." The unemployed steelworker of "Youngstown" left the Monongahela Valley and became "The New Timer." These last two songs, along with "The Ghost of Tom Joad," chronicled the increasing economic division of the '80s and '90s and the hard times and consequences for many of the people whose work and sacrifice helped build the country we live in.

With tour director George Travis

A lot of the songs on *The Ghost of Tom Joad* have settings in the Southwest. I'd been through the Central Valley many times on the way to visiting my parents. I'd often stop and spend some time in the small farm towns off the interstate. But it still took a good amount of research to get the details of the region correct. I traced the stories out slowly and carefully. I thought hard about who these people were and the choices they were presented with.

In California there was a sense of a new country being formed on the edge of the old. But the old stories of race and exclusion continued to be played out. I tried to catch a small piece of this on the songs I wrote for *Tom Joad*. "Sinaloa Cowboys," "The Line," "Balboa Park," and "Across the Border" were songs that traced the lineage of my earlier characters to the Mexican migrant experience in the New West. These songs completed a circle, bringing me back to 1978 and the inspiration I'd gotten from Steinbeck's *The Grapes of Wrath.* Their skin was darker and their language had changed, but these were people trapped by the same brutal circumstances.

By the end of *Tom Joad,* I'd written about the death and personal destruction that accompany the lives of many of the people who inspired these songs. I was working on "Galveston Bay," a song that originally had a more violent ending. But it began to feel false. If I was going to find some small window of light, I had to do it with this man in this song.

I had already written "Across the Border," a song that was like a prayer or dream you have the night before you're going to take a dangerous journey. The singer seeks a home where his love will be rewarded, his faith restored, where a tenuous peace and hope may exist. With "Galveston Bay" I had to make these ideas feel attainable. The song asks the question, Is the most political act an individual one, something that happens in the dark, in the quiet, when someone makes a particular decision that affects his immediate world? I wanted a character who is driven to do the wrong thing, but does not. He instinctively refuses to add to the violence in the world around him. With great difficulty and against his own grain he transcends his circumstances. He finds the strength and grace to save himself and the part of the world he touches.

The album ends with "My Best Was Never Good Enough," which was inspired by the cliché-popping sheriff in noir writer Jim Thompson's book *The Killer Inside Me.* It was my parting joke and shot at the way pop culture trivializes complicated moral issues, how the nightly news "sound bytes" and packages life to strip away the dignity of human events.

I knew that *The Ghost of Tom Joad* wouldn't attract my largest audience. But I was sure the songs on it added up to a reaffirmation of the best of what I do. The record was something new, but it was also a reference point to the things I tried to stand for and be about as a songwriter.

the ghost of tom joad

Men walkin' 'long the railroad tracks
Goin' someplace there's no goin' back
Highway patrol choppers comin' up over
    the ridge
Hot soup on a campfire under the
    bridge

Shelter line stretchin' 'round the corner
Welcome to the new world order
Families sleepin' in their cars in the
    Southwest
No home, no job, no peace, no rest

The highway is alive tonight
But nobody's kiddin' nobody about
    where it goes
I'm sittin' down here in the campfire
    light
Searchin' for the ghost of Tom Joad

He pulls a prayer book out of his
    sleeping bag
Preacher lights up a butt and takes
    a drag
Waitin' for when the last shall be first
    and the first shall be last
In a cardboard box 'neath the under-
    pass

Got a one-way ticket to the promised
    land

You got a hole in your belly and a gun
    in your hand
Sleeping on a pillow of solid rock
Bathin' in the city aqueduct

The highway is alive tonight
Where it's headed everybody knows
I'm sittin' down here in the campfire
    light
Waitin' on the ghost of Tom Joad

Now Tom said "Mom, wherever there's a
    cop beatin' a guy
Wherever a hungry newborn baby cries
Where there's a fight 'gainst the blood
    and hatred in the air
Look for me, Mom, I'll be there
Wherever there's somebody fightin' for a
    place to stand
Or decent job or a helpin' hand
Wherever somebody's strugglin' to be
    free
Look in their eyes, Mom, you'll see me"

Well the highway is alive tonight
But nobody's kiddin' nobody about
    where it goes
I'm sittin' down here in the campfire
    light
With the ghost of old Tom Joad

straight time

Got out of prison back in '86 and I
    found a wife
Walked the clean and narrow
Just tryin' to stay out and stay alive
Got a job at the rendering plant, it ain't
    gonna make me rich
In the darkness before dinner comes
Sometimes I can feel the itch
I got a cold mind to go tripping 'cross
    that thin line
I'm sick of doin' straight time

My uncle's at the evenin' table, makes
    his living runnin' hot cars
Slips me a hundred-dollar bill says
"Charlie you best remember who your
    friends are"
Got a cold mind to go tripping 'cross
    that thin line
I ain't makin' straight time

Eight years in it feels like you're gonna
    die

But you get used to anything
Sooner or later it just becomes your life

Kitchen floor in the evening tossin' my
    little babies high
Mary's smiling but she's watching me
    out of the corner of her eye
Seems you can't get any more than
    half free
I step out onto the front porch and suck
    the cold air deep inside of me
Got a cold mind to go tripping 'cross
    that thin line
I'm sick of doin' straight time

In the basement, huntin' gun and a
    hacksaw
Sip a beer and thirteen inches of barrel
    drop to the floor
Come home in the evening, can't get
    the smell from my hands
Lay my head down on the pillow
And go driftin' off into foreign lands

highway 29

I slipped on her shoe, she was a perfect
    size seven
I said "There's no smokin' in the store,
    ma'am"
She crossed her legs and then
We made some small talk, that's where
    it should have stopped
She slipped me her number, I put it in
    my pocket
My hand slipped up her skirt, every-
    thing slipped my mind
In that little roadhouse
On Highway 29

It was a small-town bank, it was a
    mess
Well I had a gun, you know the rest
Money on the floorboards, shirt was
    covered in blood
And she was cryin', her and me we
    headed south
On Highway 29

In a little desert motel the air was hot
    and clean
I slept the sleep of the dead, I didn't
    dream

I woke in the morning, washed my face
    in the sink
We headed into the Sierra Madres
    'cross the border line
The winter sun shot through the black
    trees
I told myself it was all something in her
But as we drove I knew it was some-
    thing in me
Something that'd been comin' for a
    long long time
And something that was here with me
    now
On Highway 29

The road was filled with broken glass
    and gasoline
She wasn't sayin' nothin', it was just a
    dream
The wind come silent through the wind-
    shield
All I could see was snow, sky and pines
I closed my eyes and I was runnin'
I was runnin', then I was flyin'

Youngstown

Here in northeast Ohio
Back in 1803
James and Dan Heaton
Found the ore that was linin' Yellow
   Creek
They built a blast furnace
Here along the shore
And they made the cannonballs
That helped the Union win the war

Here in Youngstown
Here in Youngstown
My sweet Jenny I'm sinkin' down
Here darlin' in Youngstown

Well my daddy worked the furnaces
Kept 'em hotter than hell
I come home from 'Nam, worked my way
   to scarfer
A job that'd suit the devil as well
Taconite, coke and limestone
Fed my children and made my pay
Them smokestacks reachin' like the
   arms of God

Into a beautiful sky of soot and clay

Here in Youngstown
Here in Youngstown
Sweet Jenny I'm sinkin' down
Here darlin' in Youngstown

Well my daddy come on the Ohio works
When he come home from World War
   Two
Now the yard's just scrap and rubble
He said "Them big boys did what Hitler
   couldn't do"
These mills they built the tanks and
   bombs
That won this country's wars
We sent our sons to Korea and Vietnam
Now we're wondering what they were
   dyin' for

Here in Youngstown
Here in Youngstown
My sweet Jenny I'm sinkin' down
Here darlin' in Youngstown

From the Monongahela Valley
To the Mesabi iron range
To the coal mines of Appalachia
The story's always the same
Seven hundred tons of metal a day
Now sir you tell me the world's changed
Once I made you rich enough
Rich enough to forget my name

And Youngstown
And Youngstown
My sweet Jenny I'm sinkin' down
Here darlin' in Youngstown

When I die I don't want no part of
   heaven
I would not do heaven's work well
I pray the devil comes and takes me
To stand in the fiery furnaces of hell

sinaloa cowboys

Miguel came from a small town in
  northern Mexico
He came north with his brother Luis to
  California three years ago
They crossed at the river levee when
  Luis was just sixteen
And found work together in the fields of
  the San Joaquin

They left their homes and family
Their father said "My sons one thing
  you will learn
For everything the North gives it exacts
  a price in return"
They worked side by side in the
  orchards
From morning till the day was through
Doing the work the *hueros* wouldn't do
Word was out some men in from

Sinaloa were looking for some hands
Well deep in Fresno county there was a
  deserted chicken ranch
There in a small tin shack on the edge
  of a ravine
Miguel and Luis stood cooking
  methamphetamine

You could spend a year in the orchards
Or make half as much in one ten-hour
  shift
Working for the men from Sinaloa
But if you slipped
The hydriodic acid could burn right
  through your skin
They'd leave you spittin' up blood in the
  desert
If you breathed those fumes in

It was early one winter evening as
  Miguel stood watch outside
When the shack exploded lighting up
  the valley night
Miguel carried Luis's body over his
  shoulder
Down a swale to the creekside
And there in the tall grass Luis Rosales
  died
Miguel lifted Luis's body into his truck
  and then he drove
To where the morning sunlight fell on a
  eucalyptus grove
There in the dirt he dug up ten
  thousand dollars, all that they'd
  saved
Kissed his brother's lips and placed
  him in his grave

the line

I got my discharge from Fort Irwin
Took a place on the San Diego county
   line
Felt funny bein' a civilian again
It'd been some time
My wife had died a year ago
I was still tryin' to find my way back
   whole
Went to work for the INS on the line
With the California border patrol

Bobby Ramirez was a ten-year veteran
We became friends
His family was from Guanajuato
So the job it was different for him
He said "They risk death in the deserts
   and mountains
Pay all they got to the smugglers' rings
We send 'em home and they come right
   back again
Carl, hunger is a powerful thing"

Well I was good at doin' what I was
   told
Kept my uniform pressed and clean
At night I chased their shadows
Through the arroyos and ravines
Drug runners, farmers with their
   families
Young women with little children by
   their sides

Come night we'd wait out in the
   canyons
And try to keep 'em from crossin' the
   line

Well the first time that I saw her
She was in the holdin' pen
Our eyes met and she looked away
Then she looked back again
Her hair was black as coal
Her eyes reminded me of what I'd lost
She had a young child cryin' in her
   arms
I asked "Señora, is there anything I can
   do?"

There's a bar in Tijuana where me and
   Bobby drink alongside
The same people we'd sent back the
   day before
We met there, she said her name was
   Luisa
She was from Sonora and had just
   come north
We danced and I held her in my arms
And I knew what I would do
She said she had some family in
   Madera County
If she, her child and younger brother
   could just get through

At night they come across the levee
In the searchlight's dusty glow
We'd rush 'em in our Broncos
Force 'em back down into the river
   below
She climbed into my truck
She leaned toward me and we kissed
As we drove her brother's shirt slipped
   open
And I saw the tape across his chest

We were just about on the highway
When Bobby's jeep come up in the dust
   on my right
I pulled over and let my engine run
And stepped out into his lights
I felt myself movin'
My gun restin' 'neath my hand
We stood there starin' at each other
As off through the arroyo she ran

Bobby Ramirez he never said nothin'
Six months later I left the line
I drifted to the central valley
And took what work that I could find
At night I searched the local bars
And the migrant towns
Lookin' for my Luisa
With the black hair fallin' down

balboa park

He laid his blanket underneath the
   freeway
As the evening sky grew dark
Took a sniff of *toncho* from his Coke can
And headed through Balboa Park
Where the men in their Mercedes
Come nightly to employ
In the cool San Diego evening
The services of the border boys

He grew up near the Zona Norte
With the hustlers and smugglers he
   hung out with
He swallowed their balloons of cocaine
Brought 'em across to the Twelfth Street
   strip
Sleeping in a shelter
If the night got too cold
Runnin' from the *migra*
Of the border patrol

Past the salvage yard 'cross the train
   tracks
And in through the storm drain
They stretched their blankets out 'neath
   the freeway
And each one took a name

There was X-man and Cochise
Little Spider his sneakers covered in river
   mud
They come north to California
End up with the poison in their blood

He did what he had to for the money
Sometimes he sent home what he could
   spare
The rest went to high-top sneakers and
   toncho
And jeans like the *gavachos* wear

One night the border patrol swept Twelfth
   Street
A big car come fast down the boulevard
Spider stood caught in its headlights
Got hit and went down hard
As the car sped away Spider held his
   stomach
Limped to his blanket 'neath the under-
   pass
Lie there tasting his own blood on his
   tongue
Closed his eyes and listened to the cars
Rushin' by so fast

dry lightning

I threw my robe on in the morning
Watched the ring on the stove turn red
Stared hypnotized into a cup of coffee
Pulled on my boots and made the bed
Screen door hangin' off its hinges
Kept bangin' me awake all night
As I look out the window
The only thing in sight
Is dry lightning on the horizon line
Just dry lightning and you on my mind

I chased the heat of her blood
Like it was the Holy Grail

Descend beautiful spirit
Into the evening pale
Her Appaloosa's
Kickin' in the corral smelling rain
There's a low thunder rolling
'Cross the mesquite plain
But there's just dry lightning on the
  horizon line
It's just dry lightning and you on my
  mind

I'd drive down to Alvarado Street
Where she'd dance to make ends meet

I'd spend the night over my gin
As she'd talk to her men
Well the piss yellow sun
Comes bringin' up the day
She said "Ain't nobody can give nobody
What they really need anyway"
Well you get so sick of the fightin'
You lose your fear of the end
But I can't lose your memory
And the sweet smell of your skin
And it's just dry lightning on the horizon
  line
Just dry lightning and you on my mind

the new timer

He rode the rails since the Great
   Depression
Fifty years out on the skids
He said "You don't cross nobody
You'll be all right out here, kid"

Left my family in Pennsylvania
Searchin' for work I hit the road
I met Frank in East Texas
In a freight yard blown through with
   snow
From New Mexico to Colorado
California to the sea
Frank he showed me the ropes, sir
Just till I could get back on my feet

I hoed sugar beets outside of Firebaugh
I picked the peaches from the
   Marysville trees
They bunked us in a barn just like
   animals

Me and a hundred others just like me

We split up come the springtime
I never seen Frank again
'Cept one rainy night he blew by me on
   a grainer
Shouted my name and disappeared in
   the rain and wind

They found him shot dead outside of
   Stockton
His body lyin' on a muddy hill
Nothin' taken, nothin' stolen
Somebody killin' just to kill
Late that summer I was rollin' through
   the plains of Texas
A vision passed before my eyes
A small house sittin' trackside
With the glow of the savior's beautiful
   light
A woman stood cookin' in the kitchen

Kid sat at a table with his old man
Now I wonder does my son miss me
Does he wonder where I am

Tonight I pick my campsite carefully
Outside the Sacramento yard
Gather some wood and light a fire
In the early winter dark

Wind whistling cold I pull my coat
   around me
Heat some coffee and stare out into the
   black night
I lie awake, I lie awake, sir
With my machete by my side

My Jesus your gracious love and mercy
Tonight I'm sorry could not fill my heart
Like one good rifle
And the name of who I ought to kill

across the border

Tonight my bag is packed
Tomorrow I'll walk these tracks
That will lead me across the border

Tomorrow my love and I
Will sleep 'neath auburn skies
Somewhere across the border

We'll leave behind, my dear
The pain and sadness we found here
And we'll drink from the Bravo's muddy
    water

Where the sky grows gray and wide
We'll meet on the other side
There across the border

For you I'll build a house
High upon a grassy hill
Somewhere across the border

Where pain and memory
Pain and memory have been stilled
There across the border

And sweet blossoms fill the air
Pastures of gold and green
Roll down into cool clear waters

And in your arms 'neath open skies
I'll kiss the sorrow from your eyes
There across the border

Tonight we'll sing the songs
I'll dream of you, my *corazón*
And tomorrow my heart will be strong

And may the saints' blessing and grace
Carry me safely into your arms
There across the border

For what are we
Without hope in our hearts
That someday we'll drink from God's
    blessed waters

And eat the fruit from the vine
I know love and fortune will be mine
Somewhere across the border

galveston bay

For fifteen years Le Bin Son
Fought side by side with the Americans
In the mountains and deltas of Vietnam
In '75 Saigon fell and he left his
   command
And brought his family to the promised
   land

Seabrook, Texas and the small towns in
   the Gulf of Mexico
It was Delta country and reminded him
   of home
He worked as a machinist, put his money
   away
And bought a shrimp boat with his
   cousin
And together they harvested Galveston
   Bay

In the mornin' 'fore the sun come up
He'd kiss his sleepin' daughter
Steer out through the channel
And cast his nets into the water

Billy Sutter fought with Charlie Company
In the highlands of Quang Tri
He was wounded in the battle of Chu Lai
Shipped home in '68

There he married and worked the Gulf
   fishing grounds
In a boat that'd been his father's
In the morning he'd kiss his sleeping
   son
And cast his nets into the water

Billy sat in front of his TV as the South
   fell
And the communists rolled into Saigon
He and his friends watched as the
   refugees came
Settled on the same streets and worked
   the coast they'd grew up on
Soon in the bars around the harbor was
   talk
Of America for Americans
Someone said "You want 'em out, you
   got to burn 'em out"
And brought in the Texas Klan

One humid Texas night there were three
   shadows on the harbor
Come to burn the Vietnamese boats
   into the sea
In the fire's light shots rang out
Two Texans lay dead on the ground
Le stood with a pistol in his hand

A jury acquitted him in self-defense
As before the judge he did stand
But as Le walked down the courthouse
   steps
Billy said "My friend, you're a dead
   man"

One late summer night Le stood watch
   along the waterside
Billy stood in the shadows
His K-bar knife in his hand
And the moon slipped behind the
   clouds
Le lit a cigarette, the bay was still
   as glass
As he walked by Billy stuck his knife
   into his pocket
Took a breath and let him pass

In the early darkness Billy rose up
Went into the kitchen for a drink of
   water
Kissed his sleeping wife
Headed into the channel
And cast his nets into the water
Of Galveston Bay

my best was never good enough

"Every cloud has a silver lining, every
  dog has his day"
She said "Now don't say nothin'
If you don't have something nice to say
The tough now they get going when the
  going gets tough"
But for you my best was never good
  enough

"Now don't try for a home run baby
If you can get the job done with a hit
Remember a quitter never wins
And a winner never quits
The sun don't shine on a sleepin' dog's
  ass"

And all the rest of that stuff
But for you my best was never good
  enough

"If God gives you nothin' but lemons
  then you make some lemonade
The early bird catches the fuckin' worm,
  Rome wasn't built in a day
Now life's like a box of chocolates
You never know what you're going to get
Stupid is as stupid does" and all the
  rest of that shit
Come on pretty baby call my bluff
'Cause for you my best was never good
  enough

acknowledgments

'd like to thank all those who worked alongside me in bringing my songs to life, particularily Jon Landau, my good friend and longtime working partner, with whom over the years I've discussed many of the issues and ideas that mattered to me and became central to my work; members of the E Street Band—Roy Bittan, Ernest Carter, Clarence Clemons, Danny Federici, Nils Lofgren, Vini Lopez, David Sancious, Patti Scialfa, Garry Tallent, Steve Van Zandt, and Max Weinberg—whose contributions and performance of my music expanded its boundaries and power; and all the other musicians whose efforts graced my work. I'd also like to thank Chuck Plotkin and Toby Scott for shepherding my songs through the recording process; and Barbara Carr and everyone at Landau Management. Thanks also to our publisher, Avon Books, especially Lou Aronica; David Gorman

and his talented production team; and Anne Marie Spagnuolo.

The idea for this book began with Sandy Choron. Her dedication and resilience, as well as that of Harry Choron, through its many incarnations is greatly appreciated. I'd like to thank Bob Santelli for the time we spent together shaping the short pieces that preface each album section. His hard work and companionship made a difficult process enjoyable.

Finally, I'd like to thank my family for their love and patience, and the fans for taking my songs into their lives and making them theirs.

index of song titles

index of first lines

298

credits

photographs

Mary Alfieri: xii, 20, 24, 36-37
Edie Baskin: 102
Joel Bernstein: 97, 99, 114-15, 120-21
Phil Ceccola: 23, 27, 28
Peter Cunningham: 13
Matt DiLea: 306
Tony DiLea: 243, 253
David Gahr: 22
Lynn Goldsmith: 163, 165
Todd Kaplan: 202
David Kennedy: 132, 134, 135, 142, 147, 150-51, 175
Annie Leibovitz: 160, 168, 178-79, 186, 188, 192, 208-09, 225, 244-45
Fred Lombardi: 4, 8
Jim Marchese: 94, 96, 111, 122, 129, 162, 166
Eric Meola: 40-41
Hart Perry: 6
Neal Preston: 214, 217, 218, 261, 272, 292
Barbara Pyle: 26, 43, 45, 47, 48, 53, 56-57, 60, 65
Herb Ritts: 234
David Rose: 219, 238, 258, 260, 269, 273, 275
Adele Springsteen: 2
Bruce Springsteen, 3
Pam Springsteen: 189, 190, 201, 205, 216, 220, 240, 250-51, 256, 270, 278, 285, 289, 294
Frank Stefanko: 62, 64, 67, 68, 72-73, 92, 156-57
Timothy White: 212, 215

songs

"Blinded by the Light" ©1972 Bruce Springsteen (ASCAP)
"Growin' Up" ©1972 Bruce Springsteen (ASCAP)
"Mary Queen of Arkansas" ©1972 Bruce Springsteen (ASCAP)
"Does This Bus Stop at 82nd Street?" ©1972 Bruce Springsteen (ASCAP)
"Lost in the Flood" ©1972 Bruce Springsteen (ASCAP)
"The Angel" ©1972 Bruce Springsteen (ASCAP)
"For You" ©1972 Bruce Springsteen (ASCAP)
"Spirit in the Night" ©1972 Bruce Springsteen (ASCAP)
"It's Hard to Be a Saint in the City" ©1972 Bruce Springsteen (ASCAP)
"The E Street Shuffle" ©1973 Bruce Springsteen (ASCAP)
"4th of July, Asbury Park (Sandy)" ©1973 Bruce Springsteen (ASCAP)
"Kitty's Back" ©1973 Bruce Springsteen (ASCAP)
"Wild Billy's Circus Story" ©1973 Bruce Springsteen (ASCAP)
"Incident on 57th Street" ©1973 Bruce Springsteen (ASCAP)
"Rosalita (Come Out Tonight)" ©1973 Bruce Springsteen (ASCAP)
"New York City Serenade" ©1973 Bruce Springsteen (ASCAP)
"Thunder Road" ©1975 Bruce Springsteen (ASCAP)
"Tenth Avenue Freeze-out" ©1975 Bruce Springsteen
"Night" ©1975 Bruce Springsteen (ASCAP)
"Backstreets" ©1975 Bruce Springsteen (ASCAP)
"Born to Run" ©1975 Bruce Springsteen (ASCAP)
"She's the One" ©1975 Bruce Springsteen (ASCAP)
"Meeting Across the River" ©1975 Bruce Springsteen (ASCAP)
"Jungleland" ©1975 Bruce Springsteen (ASCAP)
"Badlands" ©1978 Bruce Springsteen (ASCAP)
"Adam Raised a Cain" ©1978 Bruce Springsteen (ASCAP)
"Something in the Night" ©1978 Bruce Springsteen (ASCAP)
"Candy's Room" ©1978 Bruce Springsteen (ASCAP)
"Racing in the Street" ©1978 Bruce Springsteen (ASCAP)
"The Promised Land" ©1978 Bruce Springsteen (ASCAP)
"Factory" ©1978 Bruce Springsteen (ASCAP)
"Streets of Fire" ©1978 Bruce Springsteen (ASCAP)
"Prove It All Night" ©1978 Bruce Springsteen (ASCAP)
"Darkness on the Edge of Town" ©1978 Bruce Springsteen (ASCAP)
"The Ties That Bind" ©1980 Bruce Springsteen (ASCAP)
"Sherry Darling" ©1980 Bruce Springsteen (ASCAP)
"Jackson Cage" ©1980 Bruce Springsteen (ASCAP)
"Two Hearts" ©1980 Bruce Springsteen (ASCAP)
"Independence Day" ©1980 Bruce Springsteen (ASCAP)
"Hungry Heart" ©1980 Bruce Springsteen (ASCAP)
"Out in the Street" ©1980 Bruce Springsteen (ASCAP)
"Crush on You" ©1980 Bruce Springsteen (ASCAP)
"You Can Look (But You Better Not Touch)" ©1980 Bruce Springsteen (ASCAP)
"I Wanna Marry You" ©1980 Bruce Springsteen (ASCAP)
"The River" ©1980 Bruce Springsteen (ASCAP)
"Point Blank" ©1980 Bruce Springsteen (ASCAP)
"Cadillac Ranch" ©1980 Bruce Springsteen (ASCAP)
"I'm a Rocker" ©1980 Bruce Springsteen (ASCAP)
"Fade Away" ©1980 Bruce Springsteen (ASCAP)
"Stolen Car" ©1980 Bruce Springsteen (ASCAP)
"Ramrod" ©1980 Bruce Springsteen (ASCAP)
"The Price You Pay" ©1980 Bruce Springsteen (ASCAP)
"Drive All Night" ©1980 Bruce Springsteen (ASCAP)
"Wreck on the Highway" ©1980 Bruce Springsteen (ASCAP)
"Nebraska" ©1982 Bruce Springsteen (ASCAP)
"Atlantic City" ©1982 Bruce Springsteen (ASCAP)
"Mansion on the Hill" ©1982 Bruce Springsteen (ASCAP)
"Johnny 99" ©1982 Bruce Springsteen (ASCAP)
"Highway Patrolman" ©1982 Bruce Springsteen (ASCAP)
"State Trooper" ©1982 Bruce Springsteen (ASCAP)
"Used Cars" ©1982 Bruce Springsteen (ASCAP)
"Open All Night" ©1982 Bruce Springsteen (ASCAP)
"My Father's House" ©1982 Bruce Springsteen (ASCAP)
"Reason to Believe" ©1982 Bruce Springsteen (ASCAP)
"Born in the U.S.A." ©1984 Bruce Springsteen (ASCAP)

"Cover Me" ©1982 Bruce Springsteen (ASCAP)
"Darlington County" ©1984 Bruce Springsteen (ASCAP)
"Working on the Highway" ©1984 Bruce Springsteen (ASCAP)
"Downbound Train" ©1984 Bruce Springsteen (ASCAP)
"I'm on Fire" ©1984 Bruce Springsteen (ASCAP)
"No Surrender" ©1984 Bruce Springsteen (ASCAP)
"Bobby Jean" ©1984 Bruce Springsteen (ASCAP)
"I'm Goin' Down" ©1984 Bruce Springsteen (ASCAP)
"Glory Days" ©1984 Bruce Springsteen (ASCAP)
"Dancing in the Dark" ©1984 Bruce Springsteen (ASCAP)
"My Hometown" ©1984 Bruce Springsteen (ASCAP)
"Ain't Got You" ©1987 Bruce Springsteen (ASCAP)
"Tougher Than the Rest" ©1987 Bruce Springsteen (ASCAP)
"All That Heaven Will Allow" ©1987 Bruce Springsteen (ASCAP)
"Spare Parts" ©1987 Bruce Springsteen (ASCAP)
"Cautious Man" ©1987 Bruce Springsteen (ASCAP)
"Walk Like a Man" ©1987 Bruce Springsteen (ASCAP)
"Tunnel of Love" ©1987 Bruce Springsteen (ASCAP)
"Two Faces" ©1987 Bruce Springsteen (ASCAP)
"Brilliant Disguise" ©1987 Bruce Springsteen (ASCAP)
"One Step Up" ©1987 Bruce Springsteen (ASCAP)
"When You're Alone" ©1987 Bruce Springsteen (ASCAP)
"Valentine's Day" ©1987 Bruce Springsteen (ASCAP)
"Human Touch" ©1992 Bruce Springsteen (ASCAP)
"Soul Driver" ©1992 Bruce Springsteen (ASCAP)
"57 Channels (And Nothin' On)" ©1992 Bruce Springsteen (ASCAP)
"Cross My Heart" ©1992 Bruce Springsteen (ASCAP) and Sonny Boy Williamson/ARC Music (BMI)
"Gloria's Eyes" ©1992 Bruce Springsteen (ASCAP)
"With Every Wish" ©1992 Bruce Springsteen (ASCAP)
"Roll of the Dice" ©1992 Bruce Springsteen (ASCAP)
"Real World" ©1992 Bruce Springsteen (ASCAP)
"All or Nothin' At All" ©1992 Bruce Springsteen (ASCAP)
"Man's Job" ©1992 Bruce Springsteen (ASCAP)
"I Wish I Were Blind" ©1992 Bruce Springsteen (ASCAP)
"The Long Goodbye" ©1992 Bruce Springsteen (ASCAP)
"Real Man" ©1992 Bruce Springsteen (ASCAP)
"Better Days" ©1992 Bruce Springsteen (ASCAP)
"Lucky Town" ©1992 Bruce Springsteen (ASCAP)
"Local Hero" ©1992 Bruce Springsteen (ASCAP)
"If I Should Fall Behind" ©1992 Bruce Springsteen (ASCAP)
"Leap of Faith" ©1992 Bruce Springsteen (ASCAP)
"The Big Muddy" ©1992 Bruce Springsteen (ASCAP)
"Living Proof" ©1992 Bruce Springsteen (ASCAP)
"Book of Dreams" ©1992 Bruce Springsteen (ASCAP)
"Souls of the Departed" ©1992 Bruce Springsteen (ASCAP)
"My Beautiful Reward" ©1992 Bruce Springsteen (ASCAP)
"The Ghost of Tom Joad" ©1995 Bruce Springsteen (ASCAP)
"Straight Time" ©1995 Bruce Springsteen (ASCAP)
"Highway 29" ©1995 Bruce Springsteen (ASCAP)
"Youngstown" ©1995 Bruce Springsteen (ASCAP)
"Sinaloa Cowboys" ©1995 Bruce Springsteen (ASCAP)
"The Line" ©1995 Bruce Springsteen (ASCAP)
"Balboa Park" ©1995 Bruce Springsteen (ASCAP)
"Dry Lightning" ©1995 Bruce Springsteen (ASCAP)
"The New Timer" ©1995 Bruce Springsteen (ASCAP)
"Across the Border" ©1995 Bruce Springsteen (ASCAP)
"Galveston Bay" ©1995 Bruce Springsteen (ASCAP)
"My Best Was Never Good Enough" ©1995 Bruce Springsteen (ASCAP)
"Streets of Philadelphia" © 1993 Bruce Springsteen (ASCAP)
"Secret Garden" © 1995 Bruce Springsteen (ASCAP)
"Murder Incorporated" © 1995 Bruce Springsteen (ASCAP)
"Blood Brothers" © 1995 Bruce Springsteen (ASCAP)
"This Hard Land" © 1995 Bruce Springsteen (ASCAP)

April 30, 1998, Asbury Park, New Jersey

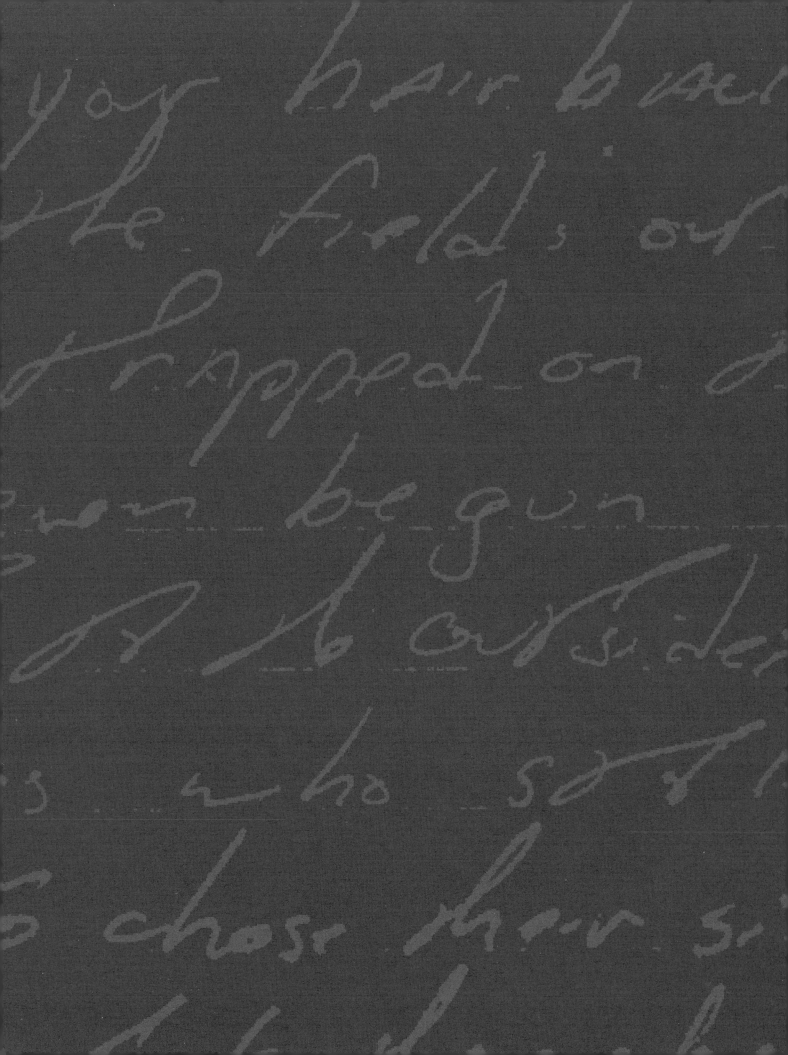